AFTER THE REVOLUTION?

AFTER THE

REVOLUTION ?

AUTHORITY IN A

GOOD SOCIETY

REVISED EDITION

ROBERT A. DAHL

YALE UNIVERSITY PRESS NEW HAVEN & LONDON

Set in Ehrhardt type by Marathon Typography Service, Durham, North Carolina.
Printed in the United States of America by Edwards Brothers, Inc.,
Ann Arbor, Michigan.

Library of Congress Cataloging-in-Publication Data
Dahl, Robert Alan, 1915–
    After the revolution? : authority in a good society / Robert A. Dahl. —
Rev. ed.
    p.   cm.
    Includes bibliographical references and index.
    ISBN 0-300-04964-1 (pbk. alk. paper)
    1. Democracy.   I. Title.
JC423.D2477   1990
321.8—dc20   90-12554
                CIP

10   9   8   7   6   5   4

CONTENTS

ACKNOWLEDGMENTS

I wish to express my appreciation to the Rockefeller Foundation and Yale University for the financial support that gave me the opportunity to write this book, and to Mrs. Marian Ash and the staff of the Yale University Press for their kind help in preparing the manuscript for publication.

Ann Sale Dahl, my wife, was particularly instrumental in persuading me to undertake this revision. Believing that *After the Revolution?* (a book that by a good margin is her favorite among my writings) was highly relevant to political developments in Eastern Europe and elsewhere, she pressed me repeatedly to consider the possibility of another edition. To her voice, Chester Kerr independently added his. As the director of the Yale University Press in 1970, he had strongly supported the publication of the original edition. The recent transformations in the Soviet Union and Eastern Europe convinced him, too, that the book had gained a new relevance. John Ryden, the present director of the Press, quickly added his enthusiasm and support, as did others at the Press, notably John Covell and Tina Weiner. Although I had been counting on a period free of publishing deadlines, the members of this formidable phalanx gained the day, and I am grateful to them for having done so.

Finally, I wish to express my appreciation to Cecile Watters, the manuscript editor for this edition.

AFTER THE REVOLUTION?

CHAPTER ONE

THREE CRITERIA

FOR AUTHORITY

n the long history of democracy few events, if any, have been more dramatic and important than the abrupt collapse of many authoritarian regimes in the 1980s and the ensuing efforts to construct democratic systems in their place.

To replace undemocratic ideas and practices with democratic institutions requires new ideas about authority and new practices. But even in countries where democratic institutions have been around for a long time not all forms of authority are necessarily democratic. Undemocratic forms of authority exist in democratic countries for at least two reasons. Even today what one ordinarily calls democracies are, as we all know, a very long way from fully democratized political systems. And in all democratic countries some kinds of organizations are explicitly and even legally governed by systems of nondemocratic authority: business firms, for example.

That democratization has never closely approached its theoretical limits, either in the government of the state or in the government of other institutions, is revealed in the three great historical movements toward democratizing the state. The first took place in Greece and Rome from about the end of the sixth century B.C. onward. In both Greece and Rome, however, democratization never went so far that the citizens outnumbered the subjects. The brilliant "democracy" of Athens was stained by slavery (and also by the exclusion of women); and in extending their dominion, the Romans never made it possible for those who could not easily get to the city of Rome to participate effectively in governing the republic. The second tide of democratization swept over the city-states of North Italy around the tenth and eleventh centuries. Although this movement helped produce some of the most beautiful town squares the world has known and proved, as Athens had earlier, that democracy is not inconsistent with beauty and magnificence in the public sector, before it had gone very far that democratic impulse ended in aristocracy, despotism, and foreign domination. Both in Greece and in North Italy, democratization was a brief, brilliant, geographically parochial movement undone by internal conflict and external subjugation.

The third movement, which it is convenient to regard as commencing with the American and French revolutions, has sought to democratize not the small city-state but the large, ultimately gigantic nation-state. If neither internal conflict nor external domination has yet written finis to this chapter, in the countries where the movement to democratize the state had made its greatest gains during the nineteenth century a kind of plateau was reached after the First World War. By then these countries—some twenty in number and all, except Japan, European or settled by European stock—had achieved executives and legislatures based on elections, a system of highly organized political parties, and universal male suffrage or something quite close to it. Although several—Italy, Germany, Austria, and Japan—suffered horrifying reversals in the 1920s and 1930s, they were restored to the now familiar plateau of political democratization as a direct consequence of the Allied victory in World War II.

Yet the plateau on which the democracies repose is obviously a long way from what a reasonable observer might regard as the summit of political democracy. In all the democratic countries it is obvious that political influence is distributed with great unevenness.

If most democrats have placed their main emphasis (rightly, I think) on democratizing the authority of the state, many have also been concerned with democratizing other social institutions where differences in power, influence, and authority are great both in magnitude and in importance. I have in mind institutions such as the political party, the economic enterprise, the trade union, the university. In these institutions democratization has not gone nearly as far as in the state. Even in institutions where the ostensible claim to legitimacy by those who wield authority is that leaders are democratically chosen, as in the political party and the trade union, everyone knows that internal democracy is mainly a fake. In the United States only one important trade union has a two-party system. Those who govern other institutions, like business firms and universities, patently do not derive their authority from democratic processes. What about those organizations so obviously crucial to large-scale democracy: political parties? In the early years of this century Robert Michels formulated the "iron law" that organization begets oligarchy to account for the acute contradiction between form and substance in the old German Social Democratic party.[1] For reasons I shall indicate in a moment, Michels's formulation is misleading. Still, his analysis is roughly correct for most political parties: typically, political parties, even in democratic countries, are far more oligarchical than democratic.

One response to the existence of undemocratic institutions in a democratic country is to demand that they be democratized. Behind this demand lies the assumption that power can be legitimate — can be considered as acceptable authority — only if it issues from fully democratic processes. Thus if political parties, for example, are oligarchical in fact, if not in form, should they not be democratized? To Americans, the answer has long been clear, it seems; and for over a century and a half we have sought to democratize our parties. That history is germane to our problem of authority.

The first national political parties in the United States — the Jeffersonian Republicans and the Federalists — were dominated by leaders in Congress abetted in the case of the Republicans by the president. Nominations for presidential and vice-presidential candidates were made by a caucus of the party's supporters in the House and Senate. Naturally, as democratic sentiments spread, this system was open to criticism; to critics it was excessively oligarchic and undemocratic. This outrage to democratic feelings was, of course, easily exploited, most notably by Andrew Jackson and his supporters; and so after 1824 the congressional nominating caucus came to an end. By 1832 it had been replaced by the most obvious alternative, a representative body democratically elected by party members — the presidential nominating convention. The convention system was soon adopted for nominating candidates for all public offices. But soon this seemingly democratic solution also proved to be illusory. Because candidates were in fact selected, in the standard phrase, by oligarchies composed of "party bosses in smoke-filled rooms," those who wanted to democratize the nominating process began to focus their attention on an even more democratic device, the direct primary. From 1901 onward the system of nominating candidates in direct primaries was widely introduced for state and congressional offices and in an increasing number of states for presidential candidates as well.

Yet even this solution failed to produce parties as democratic as some critics insisted on. Not surprisingly, the turbulent sixties led to demands for a New Politics in which the old parties would be cast aside, or if not, would become far more participatory. In response, the parties—the Democratic party, in particular—undertook further steps to expand opportunities for participation in nominations and other aspects of party governance. "From a system in which primaries played a supporting rather than a leading role," one scholar has written, "the United States rapidly moved toward a nominating system in which primaries dominated the process."[2]

So: have these recurring efforts to democratize our parties enhanced the democratic process? For example, have they improved the quality of candidates and elections? That case would be hard to make. And many political scientists believe that an increasingly plebiscitary process of nominations and elections has on balance turned out to be harmful to the democratic process.[3]

My thumbnail sketch of the evolution of American political parties suggests two preliminary conclusions. First, the democratic process in *governing a country* is not necessarily enhanced by democratizing *subsidiary parts of the process*. Government bureaus or agencies —bureaucracies, in the common parlance—provide an obvious example. It is one thing to say that people in the Internal Revenue Service ought to have *some* say over the decisions of the IRS and quite another to say that the employees of the IRS should decide whether and how they will enforce the tax laws of the United States, much less to decide what the laws should be! No matter how democratically they might decide such questions among themselves, their decisions could and probably would be in open conflict with laws passed by the Congress and the president. Do we doubt which authority should prevail? And by implication do we not insist that the Congress and the president should exercise *hierarchical* authority over the IRS? But if the only proper kind of authority in political matters is democratic, how can we justify the hierarchical authority of the Congress and the president over the employees of the IRS?

Return now to the example of political parties and the second conclusion. Earlier I said that Michels's formulation was misleading. For Michels the same forces that bring about oligarchy in political parties must also inevitably bring about oligarchy in the government of a country. For Michels, then, democracy is an impossible dream. But as later generations of political scientists began to understand, Michels made an elementary mistake. If political parties are highly *competitive*, it may not matter a great deal if they are not internally democratic or even if they are internally rather oligarchical. If parties are actively competing for votes in elections, then a party that fails to respond to majority concerns will probably lose elections, while a party that does respond to majority concerns will probably win elections. If the main reason we need political parties at all is in order for them to facilitate democracy in the *government of the country*, then might not parties that are internally oligarchic serve that purpose just as well as, or maybe better than, parties that are internally more or less democratic?

"More or less democratic"—perhaps rather less than more. Despite efforts extending back to the early decades of the Republic, American parties have stubbornly resisted all attempts to convert them into models of participatory democracy. Does democratic authority, then, require something that Americans are unable or unwilling to provide in the case of political parties—and perhaps in some other institutions as well?

Even in a democratic country, it appears, nondemocratic forms of authority might sometimes be tolerable, perhaps actually desirable. On what grounds, then, can we reasonably decide when democratic authority is better than nondemocratic authority? In pondering this question I find that I have three main criteria for judging whether I shall accept as valid and rightful, and therefore binding on me, a process for making decisions on matters that affect me. First, a process may ensure that decisions correspond with my own personal choice. Second, a process may ensure decisions informed by a special competence that would be less likely under alternative procedures. Third, a process may be less perfect than other alternatives according to the first two criteria but, on balance, more satisfactory simply because it economizes on the amount of time, attention, and energy I must give to it. Let me call these respectively the Criterion of Personal Choice, the Criterion of Competence, and the Criterion of Economy. They will become clearer as we proceed.

PERSONAL CHOICE

The Criterion of Personal Choice is extraordinarily compelling. It is easy to see why I should accept a decision that conforms with my own choice. But if it does not, why should I accept it? This is the crucial question. The problem is to reconcile personal choice with my nature as a social being, a characteristic I am unable to change, for if I insist upon the Criterion of Personal Choice, how can I hope to live peacefully with others? If the only decisions I am willing to accept and to abide by must be made by me in order to ensure that they conform with my personal choice, can any procedure for making decisions ever be legitimate? If so, what would such a procedure be?

These are in essence the questions with which Rousseau begins *The Social Contract*, which may serve to remind us that the answer is unlikely to be as simple as many who invoke his name seem to think.

Reflect a moment on some of the alternatives. I do not wish to be a hermit—a solution that in any case is increasingly elusive. If I wish to live among others, as I most emphatically do, then either we must all spontaneously agree all the time or we must have some way of dealing with our disagreements. The whole history of humanity, as I read it, argues against the possibility of perfect harmony. Even if

I can find a rather like-minded group of people to live with, surely we shall sometimes disagree among ourselves. What is even more certain, however harmonious *we* may be, as a group we shall sometimes disagree with some other group whose activities impinge on us. Just as I cannot be, and do not wish to be, a hermit, so a group of like-minded people rarely can and rarely will totally isolate themselves from the rest of humanity.

So then: I accept the fact that I wish to live in an association with others and that we shall not always agree among ourselves. Yet if I disagree occasionally with *everyone* in my association, then the Criterion of Personal Choice, interpreted simplistically and literally, means either that no procedure is acceptable to me and therefore every political order for the association will be illegitimate or else that I must completely and exclusively dominate the association. But because my power as dictator would be illegitimate to everyone else who uses the Criterion of Personal Choice, either I must rule the association by naked coercion or else I must brainwash my subjects with a royal lie. Since I am only one person, however, I cannot rule many people by my own naked force. What is more, if we all try to coerce one another, then the life of man, as Hobbes said, will be solitary, poor, nasty, brutish, and short.

The royal lie, on the other hand, requires two truths: an esoteric truth for me (the Criterion of Personal Choice), a public truth—the royal lie—for the others. The royal lie is common enough: "I am divinely appointed," or "We follow the true will of all, even if the people do not know it." Thus, Chief Leabua Jonathan, prime minister of Lesotho, arrests the man who has apparently defeated him in an election, declares a state of emergency, imposes a dusk-to-dawn curfew, rules by decree, and announces, "I have seized power and I am not ashamed of it. It may appear undemocratic in other circles, but in my conscience I know that the majority of the people are behind me."[4] The problem of the royal lie, however, is to prevent one's subjects from discovering the discrepancy between the public "truth" and the private truth. It is doubtful whether the subjects of Chief Leabua are taken in by his royal lie any more than the subjects of King Charles I of England were taken in by his.

A solution might be easier if I could find others within the association with whom I always agree. I then become part of We, who in turn, of course, are part of the association. If We have enough strength in numbers or other resources to impose our will on the Others, then our rule will be acceptable to *us*, naturally, but not necessarily to the Others. Yet this is not a very satisfactory solution. For one thing, it is very chancy. I may not find a truly solidary We within the association. Even if I do, We may be too few or too weak to impose our will on the Others. Or our attempt to do so may create a conflict so great that the association is constantly on the verge of relapsing into Hobbes's state of nature. Thus the Criterion of Personal Choice seems to offer me only a set of evil choices: isolation, anarchy, subjection, or despotism.

If you are discouraged by this dizzy slalom from the audacious start down the slippery slope of logic to an awkward and unworthy conclusion: take courage! Rousseau began at the same place, but he did not arrive at the same end, for I did what Rousseau did not. The direction of my plunge was determined by the egoistic assumption that the Criterion of Personal Choice is valid for me but not for others. Suppose, instead, that our objective is to find a regime that according to the Criterion of Personal Choice is acceptable not only to me but to all the others in our association as well—a regime, then, which I, We, and the Others will *all* regard as legitimate.

This is the problem Rousseau set for himself at the outset of *The Social Contract*. He succeeded brilliantly—and yet so ambiguously that his solution has sometimes been interpreted (or rather misinterpreted) as a justification for a willing obedience to an omnipotent state that expresses (whatever you may happen to think about it) your *real* will or interests. In proceeding toward this new objective, then, I shall not try to follow Rousseau. I wish only to see whether, starting from his point of departure, one can arrive at his objective.

You may not have paid enough attention to the fact that we have now slipped in an additional principle: that the Criterion of Personal Choice must hold for *everyone* in the association. I think we might properly call this a preliminary version of political equality. In introducing the idea of political equality we are for the first time moving toward a central theme in these essays, namely *democratic* authority. Even if authority can be applied equally without being democratic, no authority can be democratic unless it is based on some principle of political equality.

This principle can be stated in several ways depending on the particular aspect of the underlying notion we want to emphasize. The version we reached a moment ago is that the Criterion of Personal Choice must hold for everyone in the association. We came to that conclusion as a way around a set of repugnant alternatives — isolation, anarchy, subjection, despotism. To avoid these alternatives I cannot insist on my exclusive claim to my own personal choices. Consequently, I had better recognize that others also have a right to use the Criterion of Personal Choice in judging whether decisions affecting them are valid. (Just who these "others" are conceals an intriguing and formidable problem that I shall discuss in chapter 2.)

My ground for adopting the principle, then, is rational self-interest. I cannot satisfactorily gain my own ends unless I allow others an opportunity to pursue their ends on an equal basis. Therefore we all agree that, with respect to certain matters, decisions must be made in such a way as to give equal weight to the personal choices of everyone.

To adopt such a noble principle on so egocentric a ground may strike you as unworthy. You may prefer some other basis. As even the most cursory inspection of the history of political ideas will reveal, in one form or another the principle of political equality has been justified on many different grounds. Many of these are perfectly consistent with one another and with the reason I just gave, and I would not reject a reasonable defense of the principle on any ground. Unfortunately, however, an adequate exploration of the concept and its wide-ranging ramifications would require a volume, or at least a chapter, and I do not want to undertake that task in this brief book. Instead, I am going to take the risk that most of my readers are already predisposed to accept the principle on the ground I suggested or on some other. Those who reject it entirely will, I suppose, reject a good deal of what I have to say in the rest of this book — though I hope they will read on, nonetheless.

If you are now convinced that the principle of political equality is the only reasonable way out for one who wants to escape from our set of evil choices, I have been, alas, more persuasive than I intended, for this is not the case. Just suppose that Jones, Smith, and Green are all involved in a matter about which, as they all agree, there are clearly definable differences in competence. They are, for example, Dr. Jones, Nurse Smith, and poor Mr. Green who needs open-heart surgery. I think they would all be inclined to reject political equality in the operating room and instead give a decisive voice to Dr. Jones. There are, then, matters on which we may quite rationally want to give to persons we agree are more competent a good deal more weight, perhaps even a decisive voice, in decisions within their sphere of competence. It appears to be the case, then, that a condition for my adopting the principle of political equality is my belief that, on those matters with which the particular association is concerned, all the members are pretty nearly equal in their competence. Or, to put it rather more negatively, there are not such large and well-defined differences in competence that we want to risk granting extra weight in decisions to the supposed experts. (We have not seen the last of this problem of competence. I shall return to it in the next section.)

Now among political equals, the usual way to solve a conflict requiring a collective decision is to adopt the alternative preferred by the largest number of persons—in some cases, to be sure, only if the largest number is also greater than some fraction such as one-half, two-thirds, three-quarters. There are problems with this solution, but whenever people come to look upon one another as political equals, they are driven inexorably, I think, to accept some formulation of the majority principle. One might even put it the other way round. A collection of people who accept the principle of majority decision making thereby signify their willingness to treat one another as political equals.

Does the majority principle reconcile the Criterion of Personal Choice with my destiny as a social being, my need to live among others, my desire to avoid isolation, anarchy, subjection, or despotism? This is not the place to go into all the problems raised by the majority principle. Given only one condition, however, the reconciliation seems to me pretty complete: complete enough, anyway, for everyone who does not demand absolutely flawless perfection before accepting the legitimacy of any political system. If I employ the Criterion of Personal Choice, I can hardly be expected to support the principle of majority rule in an association where I am often in the minority on decisions that adversely affect my life and well-being in a crucial way. Looked at from the perspective of the individual, then, the Criterion of Personal Choice is reconciled with the majority principle if on crucial questions my choice concurs with the majority decision. Looked at from a more general perspective, there must be a fairly high degree of agreement, or consensus, among all the members of the association. I do not think it would be fruitful to try to specify more precisely here how complete that consensus should be. At the limit, it is obvious that perfect consensus would provide a perfect reconciliation of personal choice and majority rule, since every majority would express the will of all. (This was the condition, I think, that to Rousseau made the general will identical with the will of all.) The more the association recedes from that limit, the larger the minority is or the greater the intensity of its dislike for the policies of the majority. Even so, were I that soulless character so much admired by practitioners of the dismal science, the completely rational man, it would be reasonable for me to retain my membership in the association and to accept its obligations as long as, on balance, my gains when I am in the majority exceed my losses when I am in the minority. Incidentally, the Criterion of Economy asserts itself here.

But what am I to do when this point is passed? In particular, what shall I do if I expect to be frequently in the minority on decisions that run profoundly counter to my most important choices?

There are matters that even those of us devoutly committed to the principle of political equality want to be sure that no majority will tamper with. These include those minimal freedoms necessary to protect the opportunity for those in a minority to persuade others and thereby to grow into a majority: necessary, then, to the continuing operation of the majority principle itself. You may also want these minimal freedoms—to speak, publish, assemble, and the like

—effectively protected from the reach of any majority because you regard them as good in themselves or because they are instrumental for good ends other than, and in addition to, the continuing operation of the majority principle.

You may, and very likely do, regard still other things as too precious to be at the disposal of majorities. It may be that freedom of religion can be justified as directly or indirectly necessary to the operation of the majority principle, but I doubt whether you would be content with so fragile a justification. No, the right to have some protected space around your ethical, moral, or religious commitments is, I imagine, as fundamental in its intrinsic importance to you as any political right, perhaps more so. Indeed, whatever you regard as a part of the most precious essence of the self—*your* self—is a matter you are likely to deny any government the right to invade, no matter how "democratic" it may be. If the government tries to do so, you will evade the law, as most non-Catholics and many Catholics did for many decades in the state of Connecticut before a state law banning the use of contraceptive devices was ruled unconstitutional. If you cannot evade the law, and if there are enough others like you, you will fight. In many countries the right to be schooled in one's mother tongue and to use it on a plane of equality with other languages is a matter as explosive as religion. Wherever linguistic differences are rooted in tradition, as in Canada, Belgium, Switzerland, India, and literally dozens of other countries, linguistic minorities insist on the right to their own language. To deny this right would, and often does, produce violence: repression could easily lead to civil war. Language, after all, is deeply embedded in the inner recesses of one's personality: to say that the language of my people is inferior to yours is to say that my people are inferior to yours. Because immigrants came to American shores for the most part poor and powerless, and pathetically eager to be Americans, the English-speaking majority was able to force them into a kind of linguistic homogenization. We shall never know how much damage to self-esteem they and their children suffered.

What am I to do if believing in political equality I do not wish to impose my politics by force on an unwilling majority, and yet I also fear that a majority of my association will all too readily invade domains of choice so important to me that I could not willingly accept their decisions? I do not know how many solutions there may be to this problem, but let me suggest several that are particularly relevant to our subject. Perhaps the most familiar—to Americans certainly—is to see if the members of my association can agree that these matters are to be put sufficiently out of reach of ordinary majorities so that I am adequately protected.

There are a number of reasons members might rationally agree to a limitation of some kind on the power of majorities: to ensure that a minority will join the association, to preserve the association from disruption, to keep the loyalty and support of a minority, because many members of the putative majority may anticipate that they may sometimes be in a minority on the same kind of matter and therefore need the same protection, because they distrust their own power to act wisely without some constraints, because they can trade their concession on this matter for guarantees on something else, and so on.

What constitutes a satisfactory guarantee will vary. We may agree that the matter to be protected is absolutely beyond regulation by the state, for example, or that a qualified majority is required, or that my minority shall have a veto. Our agreement may be embodied as an article in a written constitution, as an explicit compact outside the constitution, as an informal understanding, or in other ways. Let me call this solution a system of Mutual Guarantees.

Frequently, of course, mutual agreement is impossible. In that case, if I remain in the association—and I may feel compelled to do so for a number of reasons—I may soon find myself deprived of a personal choice on a matter of critical importance to me and, as a result, come to consider the decisions of the association, at least on this matter, as purely coercive and without moral sanction. I may obey, but more out of fear than moral choice. Given the opportunity, I shall, in fact, probably disobey.

Now I could regain my opportunity to effectuate my personal choices if, by forming a new association exclusively with my cobelievers, I were able to eliminate any conflict between myself and the majority. In an association in which all the members agree, there being no majority or minority, our problem vanishes. As I suggested a moment ago, this state of perfect consensus may be thought of as a kind of limit at which the reconciliation of personal choice with political equality and majority rule is perfect. The closer our association approaches that limit, the more complete is the reconciliation. Consequently, if people with different views were allowed to sort themselves out into different and entirely homogeneous and consensual associations, each of us would exist in a harmonious association where we had nothing to fear from the majority: where, as a matter of fact, any majority would express the will of all of us, except when the members of a majority, not being soulless rational beings, occasionally erred because of impulse, lack of reflection, or ignorance.

If these separate associations were little city-states, it might not be stretching things too much to call this Rousseau's solution. But you have probably also thought of the analogy with religious toleration where coreligionists band together in autonomous associations and in case of internal conflict disband, divide, or secede to form new and more like-minded associations. There are implications here, as we are going to see, that will draw us further and further away from Rousseau. So let me call this solution — we need a handy label for it during our discussion — the solution of Consensual Associations.

It is possible to reduce or eliminate conflict within an association between a minority and a majority in other ways than forming separate associations: by arbitration or adjudication, for example. There is, however, a general class of possibilities so important to our discussion that it is worth emphasizing: sometimes a matter about which we disagree can be turned over so completely to the domain of personal choice that no generally binding decision is required. Two familiar issues of this kind are the religious instruction, if any, to be given one's own children and whether they are to be educated in public or private schools. Some years ago the Supreme Court of the United States affirmed that the use of contraceptive devices falls in this domain. One might call this alternative a solution by Autonomous Decisions. For reasons that will be obvious it might also be called Consumers' Choice.

Judgments as to the appropriate domain of Autonomous Decisions are constantly changing. Efforts to define the domain once and for all have always failed. Thus in the United States, owning and driving a machine that emits exhaust fumes has been rapidly moving out of the domain of Autonomous Decisions to regulation by collective decision (though not, I must say, rapidly enough for some of us), and sexual practices among consenting adults are moving from collective regulation to the domain of individual choice.

One significant area of personal decision is personal consumption. To decide by majority vote what each member of an association is allowed to consume might be possible in very small and highly consensual groups where there is very little to consume. In any other circumstances, the system would be either catastrophic or unenforceable: that is, it would produce either chaos or black markets.

Under certain conditions, which economists are fond of describing to us, prices and allocations may be made to respond with sensitivity to consumers' choices. A theoretical system of this kind is often called *consumer sovereignty*. People may and do disagree as to just what items should be placed within the domain of consumer sovereignty, particularly when incomes are distributed as unequally as in the United States. If incomes were substantially equal, surely most of us would say: clothing and food, yes, but the sale of human beings, no.

An extremely important characteristic of Autonomous Decision, or if you like, Consumers' Choice, is that by eliminating the need for a collective decision it fully honors the Criterion of Personal Choice. Why then, you may wonder, do we ever reject Autonomous Decisions in favor of collective decisions?

Before answering this question, let me swiftly retrace our steps. You will remember that the Criterion of Personal Choice seemed to plunge me at once straight into the middle of human society. I took for granted that people live in society, disagree, need means for arriving at collective decisions. I tried to show that reconciling personal choice with my desire to live among my fellows allows no easy solutions. If I also want to respect the right of others to their personal choices, if, therefore, I accept them as my political equals, there seem to be at least three possibilities: Mutual Guarantees, Consensual Associations, Autonomous Decisions. Proceeding as I did, the domain of Autonomous Decisions may seem to be a kind of residual category: it is what is left over after we have rejected the other solutions. Yet I might have begun the other way round. If the Criterion of Personal Choice is best fulfilled by Autonomous Decisions, we might give this solution a certain priority: we would turn to collective decisions only as a kind of pis aller. Both ways of proceeding, by the way, have analogies in the history of political thought. It would not be wildly improper to say that the way in which I have proceeded is analogous to that of the Greeks, with their emphasis on the notion that the polis, the collective life, is prior to humankind, in the sense that human beings are not—to use a recent cliché—*truly* human except in the presence of organized human society. To begin with the primacy of Autonomous Decisions, on the other hand, is to place us in a hypothetical state of nature and to ask, with Locke, why we should ever abandon that state of nature, a question analogous to the one I raised just a moment ago: why do we ever reject Autonomous Decisions in favor of collective decisions?

There are several reasons. For example, some of the objectives we want we cannot achieve through Autonomous Decisions because they require positive acts of social cooperation, ranging from lifting a heavy load together to preventing forest fires, pollution, and traffic accidents. The most universally recognized of these objectives is defense against aggression. Again: the more harmful to us the Autonomous Decisions of others, the more likely we are to regulate or eliminate autonomy. Racial discrimination and pollution are current examples. If we think that by his Autonomous Decision a person is very likely to do great harm to himself, we may restrict his choices, as with the consumption of addictive drugs. To anticipate the next section, when we believe that individuals are not competent to make a decision that will avoid harm to themselves or to others, we may regulate or forbid Autonomous Decisions. We do not grant children the right to decide whether or not they shall go to school.

So: we have at least three possible solutions to consider—Mutual Guarantees, Consensual Associations, Autonomous Decisions. If you reflect on these solutions for a moment, several things will become clear to you at once. To begin with, a system of Mutual Guarantees that effectively places some matters beyond the reach of ordinary majorities is, as a plain matter of fact, a characteristic of *every* national political system that we ordinarily call democratic.

To be sure, democratic countries differ in the explicitness of the guarantees and the matters they cover. At one extreme, a few countries with quite distinctive subcultures have developed elaborate systems of Mutual Guarantees to protect subcultural autonomy by granting each subculture, in effect, a veto over all policies that touch upon its interests. Consociational democracy, as these systems have been called, has grown up in order to reconcile formal political equality with subcultural differences. Consociational systems have successfully mitigated the potentially explosive effects of differences in language, religion, and local loyalties in Switzerland, religion in the Netherlands, and ideology and social class in Austria. At the opposite extreme, in a much more homogeneous country like Britain the guarantees are traditional understandings, nowhere written down in a formal constitution, doubtless sometimes not written down at all, and not so much designed to protect subcultural autonomy as the rights of individuals and minorities of all kinds. Although it is a useful legal fiction that the powers of the British Parliament are unlimited and that a majority of the House of Commons may do anything it pleases—even Bagehot's ironic reservation that it could not make a man a woman or a woman a man may not hold in this age of surgery, transplants, and hormones—everyone knows that the members of Parliament are restrained in a thousand ways by the elaborate tissue of understandings woven by history that as effectively guarantees the rights of minorities in Britain as any political system in the world.

Consensual Associations and Autonomous Decisions may at first glance seem to be alternatives to a system of Mutual Guarantees. Certainly Rousseau sometimes seems to imply that if states were Consensual Associations, Mutual Guarantees would be unnecessary. A world populated by autonomous communes or city-states, internally homogeneous and externally totally isolated from one another would, no doubt, eliminate the problem of majority domination and so the need for Mutual Guarantees. Yet a situation of this kind has never existed, except perhaps occasionally in prehistory. For six thousand years, it has been impossible. It was not possible in Rousseau's time in his native Switzerland, much less in the rest of Europe. Since his time, and particularly since the Second World War, it has become absolutely clear that no significant part of the world's population, if any at all, can exist in autonomous associations totally isolated from the possibility of severe damage from outside. Since I have already made this point and shall return to it again, let it stand for the moment without further support. What our world of communes or city-states will desperately need is what the city-states of Greece and, more than a millennium later, the city-states of the Po Valley so desperately lacked: a system of Mutual Guarantees or, if you like, a system of mutual security. A system of Mutual Guarantees does not necessarily foster homogeneous associations, but in order for homogeneous associations to coexist peacefully they must be a part of a system of Mutual Guarantees.

Nor do Autonomous Decisions provide an alternative to a system of Mutual Guarantees. To be sure, once we have agreed that a particular matter belongs within the domain of Autonomous Decisions, the possibility of conflict between minority and majority is eliminated with respect to *that matter*. But to determine what remains in or out of the domain of Autonomous Decisions requires a collective decision; decisions of this kind are often a source of very profound conflict; and they may give rise to a demand for Mutual Guarantees. On matters of crucial importance to it a minority may want to be protected against the possibility of a change in the boundaries by simple majority action. Thus in the United States it has taken a long time — and the process is not yet finished — for black people to secure guarantees that racial discrimination in education, voting, housing, and employment are not to be treated as matters of individual choice. It seems doubtful to me that these guarantees could now be eliminated without producing an armed uprising among black people.

What properly belongs within the domain of Autonomous Decisions or Consumers' Choice has been a perpetual point of controversy between majorities and minorities. The history of the displacement of laissez-faire by the regulated economy is one long catalog of such disputes, and they are all around us today. Should we legalize drugs? prohibit abortions? ban the sale of pornographic magazines? Should we forbid automobiles in the center of the city? having a firearm without a license? or, for that matter, with a license? And so on and on.

Fortunately, not all these matters are incorporated into a system of Mutual Guarantees. If they were, governments would be so paralyzed that sooner or later immobility would be transformed into executive decree, emergency rule, or dictatorship. Fortunately, too, systems of Mutual Guarantees often adapt to long-run changes of belief; there is no better symbol of this adaptation than the Supreme Court of the United States. Nonetheless, it is clear that even the domain of Autonomous Decisions may require a system of Mutual Guarantees.

Let me now recapitulate the argument. If I accept the Criterion of Personal Choice as the proper basis for authority, why should I accept a decision that does not conform with my own choice?

Since I am to live with other people, which I believe I must, and since I shall not always agree with them, which I believe is inevitable, my exclusive reliance on the Criterion of Personal Choice can lead with sinister neutrality to my own despotic rule, to my subjection by others, or to anarchy among us—not that gentle anarchism of the philosophical anarchists where each of us does peacefully and responsibly what we choose without fear of hurt or hindrance but the anarchy of loneliness, violence, disorganization, and ineffectiveness.

If, however, I believe that the personal choices of others have equal dignity with my own and that we must all therefore be counted as political equals, then I may choose to accept authority as legitimate if it expresses the personal choices of the greater number in our association.

Yet there may be matters of profound importance to me which I think a simple majority cannot be counted on to protect. Even though I accept political equality, and with it the generalized right of others to adhere, like me, to the Criterion of Personal Choice, in following that criterion I cannot accept as legitimate collective decisions that reflect the preferences of the greater number if they run counter to my most deeply cherished values.

I may be able to resolve my dilemma by adhering to a system of Mutual Guarantees that effectively restrains majorities; or by withdrawing into a more Consensual Association where, our views being harmonious, I do not fear majorities (where, in Rousseau's language, the general will expressed by a majority is always truly my own will); or by having the matter transferred to the domain of Autonomous Decisions or Consumers' Choice.

Yet because with only trivial exceptions Consensual Associations cannot be truly isolated, they require the protection provided by a system of Mutual Guarantees. The boundaries of the domain of Autonomous Decisions may also have to be guaranteed by mutual agreement. In fact, what a system of Mutual Guarantees ordinarily does is to place certain matters outside the reach of ordinary majorities by placing them securely inside the domains of Consensual Associations and Autonomous Decisions.

There can be no assurance that I shall ever be able to find a satisfactory system of Mutual Guarantees: no authority, then, that I can accept as rightful. It is in any case most unlikely that any such system will ensure that I shall *always* be able to secure *my* personal choices. There are likely to be—indeed it is all but certain that there will be—some matters on which I cannot gain the guarantees I want. Moreover, other minorities may want and be able to secure guarantees that limit me when I am with the majority.

Is it irrational of me to accept a system of Mutual Guarantees that restrains me? According to the Criterion of Economy (which remains to be discussed) it is by no means irrational to accept restraints on some personal choices in order to be able to effectuate others. To the extent that I am capable of acting rationally, I will adhere to the system of Mutual Guarantees so long as the gain I expect from making some of my personal choices effective exceeds the loss I expect from the choices that I have to forgo. It may also be rational of me, of course, to work to increase the margin. Naturally, too, it may be rational to withdraw my adherence if I expect that the losses would exceed the gain. Where the balance lies, I imagine only I can judge.

COMPETENCE

If you regard a decision on some matter as binding on yourself or on other people because it is made by a person who is particularly qualified by knowledge or skill to render a correct judgment, then you accept the Criterion of Competence as an appropriate basis for authority on this matter.

There are a number of important things to notice about the Criterion of Competence. In the first place, competence takes different forms. No doubt what leaps to mind in a technological society like ours is an image of the expert in a particular "field" of knowledge whose judgments we have solid reasons to believe are better than our own—as long, that is, as she sticks to her last. These experts may be no more gifted than you or I, but by dint of study, training, and experience they know more about a particular subject than we do.

In a society oriented more toward moral concerns, the first image to occur might be that of the person of superior moral competence. Even in the United States we may conclude that a judge is not competent to sit on the Supreme Court of the United States if, though his knowledge of constitutional law is adequate, he is morally deficient. We do not want to entrust important decisions to a judge, no matter how great his grasp of the law, who has a weak hold on moral principle. Of course, as in the case of the judge, competence often requires *both* expert knowledge and moral fitness.

There are less easily defined yet undeniable forms of competence —that of the skilled performer, for example, athlete, musician, dancer, or the painter, sculptor, poet, chef.

Superior competence may be mainly a product of acquired learning or mainly a natural endowment. I doubt whether it can often be a product exclusively of one or the other. No amount of study, alas, would ever have given me the remotest approximation to the competence of a Michelangelo, a Bach, an Einstein. Yet they, too, had to acquire vast technical knowledge that was very far indeed from being present in their genes. In a less secular age, it was commonplace to explain some kinds of extraordinary competence as a product of divine intervention. Venus, who much earlier had given life to Pygmalion's Galatea, was thought by some Greeks to have lent a hand, certainly, to Phidias on the Parthenon.

In the second place, practically everyone accepts superior competence in some form or other as a requirement for making decisions on some matters. Virtually all parents seem to agree that young children are not wholly competent to decide everything for themselves: how they shall spend all their time, whether or not and when they shall go to school, see a doctor, have their teeth attended to, how much television they may watch, when they shall get up in the morning, when they must be at home, and so on. We are inclined to feel that parents fail in their duties if they do not keep poisons out of the hands of their small children or restrain them from playing in lethal places. What sort of parent would allow a one-year-old child to crawl unguarded to the edge of a waterfall? Oppression? Hardly.

The observable fact that everyone believes children are not competent to decide all questions for themselves seems innocuous enough. But take care. Once you have accepted the Criterion of Competence to justify the authority of parents or teachers over children, you are obliged to ask yourself whether there are not also great differences in competence among adults on some matters.

Two familiar examples have been used since antiquity to justify authority based on competence. These are the pilot and the physician. I am sure that I speak for most people in saying that, when I am at sea, I want the captain to be in charge. I would not want to travel on a ship where every decision was put to a vote of crew and passengers; both Competence and Economy argue against it. Nor, to update the example, would I travel on an airline that promised passengers the right to participate equally (by lot? by majority vote?) with crew and pilot in the operation of their planes. Nor would I want to be a patient in a hospital where doctors, nurses, patients, orderlies, janitors, technicians, receptionists, and the rest decided all questions on an equal basis. I should not like to be a surgical patient in an operating room governed by the principle that one person's opinion is as much entitled to a hearing as another's. I do not want to be tried in a court where every question of procedure might be appealed to a vote of judge, jury, attorneys, journalists, spectators — and defendant. I do not want a referendum to decide what drugs and food additives are safe enough to be made available to the public.

These examples suggest another point of great consequence. It is often said that everyone should have the right to participate in decisions that affect one's interests in a vital way. Yet as our examples show, the fact that decisions on some matter affect your interests in a vital way does not mean that it is necessarily rational for you to insist upon participating. On the contrary, if you believe that there are significant differences in competence with respect to some subject, the more important the decision is to you the more you should, and presumably will, try to have the decision made by the most competent authority. For your own self-interest your participation ought to stop where significant differences in competence begin.

It is precisely because human lives *are* important and because there *are* differences in competence that we want competent authorities to be in charge of the plane, the ship, the operating room. When your own life is at stake, you want the authority of the best pilot, the best physician, the best judge. If your plane or ship is hit by a hurricane, you will not, I imagine, insist that the captain consult with you and the other passengers on every decision he makes.

Is the Criterion of Competence totally at odds, then, with the Criterion of Personal Choice?

No, reflection will show that the Criterion of Competence depends in a complex way on the Criterion of Personal Choice. This dependency is clearly seen when you freely *choose* to place yourself under the authority of someone you believe to be more competent than you on some matter. When you *choose* to travel by ship or plane, you also *choose* to accept the authority of the captain—so long, at least, as he continues to demonstrate his superior competence. If you did not believe the captain was competent, you probably would not choose to travel on his ship.

Nonetheless, once you have made the choice, once you have placed yourself under the captain's jurisdiction, you are in a domain of authority subject to the competence of another and not directly or immediately to your personal choice. You might choose a fixed period of time when you will be, so to speak, within that domain. But during that time, you are under the authority of another. (If, as in the operating room, you are unconscious or irrational, you will want to be certain that a competent authority *is* in charge.)

Suppose, however, that you do not choose but are *compelled* to enter and remain against your will within the domain of this authority of superior competence. Would not the two criteria, Competence and Personal Choice, be in outright conflict, no holds barred? The child, you will say, does not always *choose* to go to school and place herself under the authority of the teacher; yet we may compel her to do so anyway. Does not the Criterion of Competence in this case totally override the Criterion of Personal Choice? Yet even here there is more than meets the eye. As any teacher will tell you, to the extent that a pupil attends from compulsion and not from choice, to that very extent the pupil rejects the authority of the teacher.

You can be compelled to obey. You cannot be compelled to believe in the superior competence of another. It is worth recalling the words Galileo is supposed to have muttered after he had signed his famous statement abjuring the heresy of believing "that the sun is the center of the world and immovable, and that the earth is not the center, and moves." *Eppur si muove*, he said—Nonetheless it moves!

Nor would Galileo have been any safer if his judges had been a majority of his fellow citizens operating according to a system of unrestrained majority rule. There is not much doubt that a majority vote taken among practically any group of ordinary Europeans in 1630 would have condemned Galileo's belief as false, for after all his theory flies directly in the face of direct observation and common sense. Indeed if his fate had depended on popular vote, he might not have gotten off as lightly as he did. *Eppur si muove!*

Now you may think that I have rather slickly shown how you can have the best of both worlds, Personal Choice and Competence. But that is not wholly possible, for in the *specific* case the two criteria often do collide, and you must choose between them. Perhaps the difference between the two can be made clear in this way. If I say that, so far as I am concerned, a process of decision making meets the Criterion of Personal Choice to perfection, I mean that the *specific* decisions resulting from the process are always identical with my expressed preferences. However, if I say that, so far as I am concerned, a process meets the Criterion of Competence perfectly, I mean that although the *specific* decisions are not necessarily identical with my expressed preferences (I may have none) and may even contradict them (if I do have any), I am nonetheless certain that they are exactly what I would want if I were competent to make specific judgments in that domain.

You can easily see that on a matter on which you do not believe yourself to be sufficiently competent, no process of decision making can completely satisfy both criteria. Often, therefore, you are compelled to choose between them. In some cases, to be sure, you might want a process that provided a mix of Personal Choice and Competence, which was not perfect according to either criterion but was satisfactory according to both and on balance better than any alternative. In other cases, however, the optimal solution might leave you with precious little room for Personal Choice or for political equality and democracy.

To make the point in a more general way, whenever you believe that X is significantly more competent than Y or Z to make a decision that will seriously affect you, you will want the decision to be made by X. You will not want it to be made by Y or Z, nor by a majority of X, Y, and Z. If X happens to be yourself, the majority principle will, I imagine, seem even more doubtful to you.

Does the Criterion of Competence, then, deal a lethal blow to the principle of political equality, and so to democracy? Just a moment ago, I showed how the Criterion of Personal Choice would in some circumstances lead you to opt for political equality and democracy as the best system for arriving at decisions in an association. Must we now conclude that, quite to the contrary, because of differences in competence there are *no* circumstances when democracy is best?

The answer is crystal clear. The Criterion of Competence is politically neutral. In itself it is neither prodemocratic nor antidemocratic. Its implications for democracy depend on one's judgment about the competence of the ordinary person.

Although the criterion itself is not antidemocratic, anyone who thinks so is. One of the minor ironies of politics is to hear those who claim to believe in democracy agreeing with their opponents that the Criterion of Competence cannot be reconciled with political equality, for it is obvious that if you think that authority based on competence is inimical to political equality and thus to democracy, then you must think that the ordinary person is incompetent.

Is the ordinary person incompetent? No judgment is more decisive for one's political philosophy. It was perhaps the single most important difference in judgment between Plato and Aristotle. If you believe, as I do, that *on the whole ordinary people are more competent than anyone else to decide when and how much they shall intervene on decisions they feel are important to them*, then you will surely opt for political equality and democracy. But if you believe that the ordinary person is less competent in this fundamental way than some particular person or minority, then I imagine that like Plato your vision of the best government is a government by this qualified person or elite.

There is not space here to deal adequately with these alternative judgments.[5] In any case, one's judgment may rest upon unarticulated premises not easily available for rational examination. Let me content myself with a few comments.

Most of the controversy over the competence of the ordinary person has, since the Greeks, focused on the realm of the state. There are good reasons for singling out the state for special attention. The state is, on the whole, the most powerful of the associations to which anyone belongs. It has a monopoly over the right to use or to control the use of coercive violence within its boundaries. If, as the Greeks thought, the well-ordered polis is a great civilizing force, the state happens to have a nasty record for being brutal, repressive, despotic, and exploitative. Even if it does not make sense for ordinary persons to try to take over the ship, the plane, or the operating room, it makes a great deal of sense for them to try to make sure that they can participate as much as they feel necessary in the affairs of the state.

Both the advocates of aristocracy, if I may use that term to cover a variety of alternatives to political equality, and the advocates of democracy must if they are honest confront some serious problems.

Advocates of aristocracy in the realm of the state face two formidable problems for neither of which, so far as I know, is there a satisfactory solution. Their minority of superior competence—the experts, wise men, guardians, or philosopher-kings—must somehow acquire and preserve both their *authority* and their *virtue*.

If, like Plato, you want the authority of your philosopher-kings to be accepted because citizens freely recognize superior competence when they see it, then you have an enormous job on your hands. I doubt whether you would seriously advocate Plato's artificial and drastic solution in *The Republic*. Plato's solution will serve as a warning to adolescents not to get too uppity, for the inauguration of the perfect republic is based upon the belief that you cannot trust anyone over ten. As Socrates puts it, the "genuine philosophers" having "come into power in a state"

> must send out into the country all citizens who are above ten years old, take over the children, away from the present habits and manners of their parents, and bring them up in their own ways under the institutions we have described. Would not that be the quickest and easiest way in which our polity could be established, so as to prosper and be a blessing to any nation in which it might arise?[6]

If your solution is not only to *impose* the rule of the elite by naked force, as Plato seemed to counsel, but also to *maintain* their rule by sheer force, as Plato was unwilling to do, then you change the whole question from one of authority, where citizens obey rulers because they believe the regime is rightful, to one of straight coercion, where citizens obey rulers because the regime is despotic. If you cannot demonstrate to me that I *should* obey your rulers, to demand that I *must* obey them is to substitute threat for reason. And then, as the saying goes, we are in a different ball game.

The members of the ruling minority also run the risk that from great exposure to temptation they may, like virgins, lose their virtue. Power may not always corrupt, but Acton was surely close to the truth in pointing out that it does have this tendency. It is all very well to start off with a wise and virtuous aristocracy; the problem is to keep it from becoming a cunning and voracious oligarchy.

A single solution to both these problems might be to allow the citizens to elect the superior minority for a fixed term of office. This solution looks so much like a prescription for representative democracy that doubtless it will frighten both the aristocrat and the democrat—the one because it concedes the need for popular sovereignty and the other because it recognizes the desirability of competent rulers.

To the advocate of aristocracy, the problem is how the philosopher-kings are to exercise authority over the rank and file. To the advocate of political equality, the problem is how the rank and file are to exercise authority over the philosopher-kings. If the first is, as I think, impossible to solve in the realm of the state, the second, though not impossible to solve in the realm of the state, is nonetheless difficult. As Rousseau rightly saw, the greater the number of citizens in the state, the more difficult the problem; for the greater the number of citizens, the greater the number of decisions that will have to be delegated to officials. It is not then utterly fanciful to suggest that *one* (but only one) function of elections in a large state is to place experts in office for a fixed term, subject to the right of citizens to protest if they dislike what the experts do and to replace them at the next election.

If you opt for political equality and democracy in the state, must you also choose these as the best basis for authority in all other associations? Again, the answer is clear: no, to insist that authority in one kind of association be democratic implies nothing about the proper basis for authority in any other association.

Let me simply remind you of the examples given earlier. One may conclude with Aristotle and against Plato that ordinary people are, everything considered, more competent to protect their own interests in the domain of the state than anyone else is and yet recognize that most of us are incompetent to run a passenger plane or a hospital. In what other matters we may be sufficiently competent to find political equality the best basis for authority, or so incompetent that we want the most qualified experts to have authority, is a question that cannot be decided once and for all. It is, rather, a question to judge from case to case.

Let me now summarize the main points I have made about the Criterion of Competence.

1. Practically everyone accepts superior competence as a criterion for making decisions on some matters.

2. The fact that decisions on some matter affect your interests in a vital way does not mean that it is necessarily rational for you to insist upon participating in these decisions. On the contrary, if significant differences in competence are involved, it may be much more rational for you to insist that the matter be decided by the most competent authority.

3. You can simultaneously adhere to both the Criterion of Competence and the Criterion of Personal Choice, without conflict between them, if no one is significantly more competent to make a decision than you, either because you are definitely the most competent or because no significant differences in competence exist with respect to the matter at hand. But if you are definitely less competent than another to make a decision on a matter, then the two criteria conflict with respect to that decision and you cannot design a system of decision making that will perfectly meet both criteria. You will have to choose. You may choose to honor one or the other exclusively, or, what is much more likely, you may try to find some optimum mix that is satisfactory by both criteria but perfect by neither.

4. The Criterion of Competence is politically neutral. In itself it is neither prodemocratic nor antidemocratic. In any association dealing with matters about which, taken all around, there are no definite and significant differences in competence among the members, the

Criterion of Competence is perfectly consistent with political equality and democracy. In fact, to the extent that each member is the best judge of what is best, the Criterion of Competence requires decision making based on equality and democracy.

5. To insist that authority be democratic in the state or some other kind of association implies nothing about the proper basis for authority in any other association. Each case requires a judgment as to the amount and significance of differences in competence among the people involved.

If you mainly agree with what I have said up to this point, we could discuss particular cases with profit, and perhaps our practical judgments would turn out to be pretty much the same. But if you have not found my argument convincing, then we would have no basis for a profitable discussion of specific cases.

ECONOMY

When you think of Athenian democracy embodied in the Assembly (*ekklesia*) which had supreme power in its monthly meetings and which all male citizens had the right and duty to attend, you may overlook the Council of Five Hundred (the *boulê*) which was chosen by lot, fifty men from each of the ten tribes. It prepared the business of the Assembly and dealt with emergencies. In addition,

> most of the administrative boards ("Government departments") were manned by members of the Boulê. But since five hundred men could not be in constant session, and were too many to make an efficient executive committee, there was an inner council, the "prytany," composed, in turn, of the fifty men drawn from each of the ten tribes, which remained in session for one-tenth of the year. Of these, one was chosen by ballot [lot] to be chairman each day.[7]

You may also overlook the fact that the Athenians elected their generals for a term of a year (and usually reelected them for additional terms).

In selecting a few among their number by lot and election to carry on when the Assembly itself could not govern, the Athenians were respecting not only the criteria of Personal Choice and Competence and the principle of political equality but also the Criterion of Economy.

When the citizens of a New England town, assembled in a town meeting, choose the town clerk and the selectmen to carry on in their behalf, they honor the Criterion of Economy. When, having grown to a population of thirty thousand they decide to replace the general town meeting with a *representative* town meeting consisting of elected representatives, they act on the Criterion of Economy. When in the course of the eighteenth century it came to be recognized that by means of elections you could join the aristocratic principle of representation to the democratic principle of political equality, democrats were exhilarated by the discovery that democracy need not after all be confined to the tiny city-state. In endorsing representative democracy, Jefferson accepted, as Rousseau did not, the Criterion of Economy.

Rationality, efficiency, economy are all different ways of speaking about essentially the same elementary thing. Rationality speaks to the unarguable notion that it is always desirable to obtain more of your values than fewer. Efficiency emphasizes the idea of gaining more output, or, if you prefer, more of what you value, for less input, that is, for less cost to what you value. Economy stresses that many of the things you value are scarce and that by wasting these scarce resources you reduce the total value of what you attain.

These terms rub many people the wrong way. Rationality sounds cerebral and lifeless. Yet rationality says nothing specific about means. It implies nothing more than that if you have an absolutely free evening in which you can paint or go to the movies, and if you really would prefer to paint, it would be absurd of you to go to the movies. Many humanists dislike the term *efficiency* because so-called efficiency experts generally seem to emphasize the wrong values. Yet consider how much better off we are in language training because of the more efficient systems for teaching languages that developed several generations ago. And would not most of us strongly favor methods of sewage disposal more efficient than polluting our rivers? If the idea of economy repels you because it sounds like a synonym for stinginess, think of human life. If you value human life, you want to be very stingy about wasting it.

Two scarce resources are so crucial to political life that I do not see how their scarcity can be ignored. These are time and effort —not least, *your* time and *your* effort. Let me concentrate on time, since I think it will serve well enough for all I want to say here.

Consider time. Without getting off into varying philosophical, poetic, or psychological characterizations of time, let us accept the palpable fact that your own time is limited. There are, as we all too frequently say, only so many hours in the day. and also in a year. or in a life. The mechanism of time is absolutely ruthless. It is implacably irreversible. Once gone, you cannot regain that lost second, minute, hour, weekend, youth, lifetime. In its interactions with space, time compels exclusion. When I write, I cannot play tennis. (It is all very well to let one's fancy loose on these matters, but the fact is that when I write I *cannot* play tennis.) Thus time insists upon sacrifice. In order to do one thing at a particular time, I am compelled to forgo doing other things. Time is of value, whether for work, play, rest, leisure, creation, puttering, loving, fighting . . .

It is rather unpleasant to think of time this way, and surely it is unhealthy to be obsessed with time. Obsession with time may cause one to waste time worrying about wasting time and to regard as time wasted what is really time well spent. It is a foolish puritanical notion that leisure time is wasted time, that fun is wasted time, that napping under a tree is wasted time.

I hope I have persuaded you that even if we ought not to be obsessed with time, a political theory must pay attention to time simply because it is valuable and scarce.

Of course, everyone really does accept this notion. Why does the New England town meeting elect a town clerk and a board of select-men? Why did the Athenians have a Council of Five Hundred, the Five Hundred an inner council of fifty, and the fifty a chairman? Above all, because of time. Townsfolk cannot be in a town meeting all the time, nor could Athenians be in Assembly all the time: evidently they thought several times a month enough. And even if the Athenians had remained in Assembly all the time, they could not have gotten through all the detailed business or managed all the affairs of the city. With a lengthy agenda, only a few people could have been allowed the time to speak on each topic; the Athenians understood that since only a few people could speak, Athens could do more honor to the principle of political equality by choosing those few by lot: hence the Five Hundred. But the Council of Five Hundred only re-created the same problem on a smaller scale, so its members delegated their authority to the fifty. But it was too much to ask the fifty to give up their time for a whole year, so the fifty changed every month. The fifty, in turn, needed a chairman, someone to make sure that they did not waste too much time on procedure: for how do you run a meeting of fifty people without a chairman unless you have an indefinite amount of time? Since the whole point of the operation was precisely to save time, to get the business of Athens done and not just talked about forever, they needed a chairman.

I had once supposed that all this was obvious; yet how many speakers I have heard who talk as if people are willing to participate in decisions without any regard for the costs of time: as if time had no value, as if attending meetings had no costs. The cost is, plainly, that the time might be used in doing something else — often, in fact, something a great deal more interesting and important than going to a meeting. Like other performers (including teachers, ministers, and actors), politicians and political activists are prone to overestimate the interest of the audience in their performance.

The amount of time devoted to making decisions is limited both by the unwillingness of the people involved to spend an inordinate amount of time on decisions and by deadlines set by events that will not wait. Because time has value, scheduled meetings often have a more or less fixed amount of time within which to do their business; the cost of not completing the agenda during that meeting is another meeting or not getting it done at all. Since events will not always wait, the calendar of events may fix the length of a meeting. The costs of further discussion may become astronomical. The Greeks being a talkative people, their captains spent a good deal of time in council wrangling about how to meet the Persian invasion. But if they had gone on debating indefinitely at Salamis, history would have taken a very different turn.

How much time will a rational person spend participating in the decisions of an association? I do not think there can be a specific answer to this question. It is possible, however, to suggest a very general answer. If time is of value, then the "cost" of using your time for one purpose is represented by the value of the most worthwhile activity you have had to give up. Suppose I have a Saturday afternoon when I can either devote my full attention to the opera on the radio, take some recreation outdoors, or work in my study. If I rank the alternatives in that order and choose to listen to the opera, then the "cost" to me of listening to the opera is to forgo being outdoors. Obviously if that cost in my view exceeds the value of listening to the opera, it would be irrational—uneconomical—to do so.

Consider now the business of participating in the decisions of an association. What it "costs" you to participate includes the value your time would have if you devoted it to the most rewarding alternative. Can we take it as axiomatic that the greater the rewards from participating, in comparison with the costs, the greater the net return from participating? And that if the gains exceed the costs it is rational for you to participate? The other side of the coin, of course, is that if the rewards do not exceed the costs, it is foolish of you to participate at all. In general, the value to you of participating in the decisions of an association is higher:

• The more you enjoy taking part. If you feel about participating in your association the way an avid amateur musician feels about playing with a group, the intrinsic rewards are high. But if your attitude is closer to that of a wife who hates camping and fishing and is being dragged off by her husband on a three-week fishing trip in the wilds, the rewards of participation are, obviously, pretty low or negative.

• The more important to you the matters the association is concerned with. An association that decides on matters of life and death is obviously worth more time than one that decides how to raise and spend funds for baseball uniforms for neighborhood children.

• The greater the difference in the alternatives at stake in the decisions of the association. If there is little difference among the alternatives before the association, you do not have much to gain from participating and might reasonably prefer to put in your time on something else.

• The more likely it is that by participating you will change the outcome in the direction of your choice. If the vote is likely to be exceedingly close, your presence is obviously more critical than if the vote is going to be overwhelming anyway. Of course, if you do not have a vote or if the voting is rigged, then your participation is worth even less.

• The more likely it is that the outcome will turn out badly if you do not participate. The converse of this is perhaps more relevant: the more likely it is that the outcome will be satisfactory to you without your involvement, the less time it is worth giving up in order to participate.

• The more competent you are with respect to the subject at hand. This may be a variant of the previous proposition, since your special competence may be necessary to ensure that a sound decision is made. Conversely, if you believe that you are not competent and will not have acquired sufficient competence by the time the decision has to be made, you might quite rationally choose not to participate in the final decision. I say "final" decision because it might be sensible of you to participate in the discussion in the hope of learning something worthwhile.

At one extreme is the inactive member of an association who does not enjoy taking part, is pretty well satisfied with the way things turn out, thinks her participation cannot change things much, sees little difference in the alternatives, does not feel very competent, and perhaps believes that what the association does is not very important anyway. To her, any time spent on the affairs of the association is bound to look like time wasted. At the other extreme is the frantic activist who would rather politic than eat, believes that the future of the world depends on her association, sees vast issues at stake in every decision, feels confident of her competence, and is equally certain not only that she can shape the outcome but that disaster will strike if she does not participate. To her, time spent on anything other than the association is time wasted.

We have all met both types, I imagine. I cannot say that one is right and the other wrong or that both are wrong and some position less extreme than either is right. The problem is much too complicated for that. You can arrive at a judgment only by examining particular cases. To make a reasoned judgment, you would have to examine each of the factors I mentioned a moment ago and keep in mind the situation of the particular person or category of persons involved. Even for a particular decision in a specific association, your judgment about the rational course of action might vary from one individual or group to another.

I know this is perplexing, but there is no help for it. When you begin to apply the Criterion of Economy to authority, you are soon driven to a discovery of very great importance: *What is an optimal system for making decisions is not necessarily what we ordinarily think of as "ideal." In fact, the optimal is almost always different from the ideal.*

When you prescribe an ideal, typically you emphasize a particular virtue—beauty, perhaps, or equality, or justice, and so on. Your ideal consists in the maximum conceivable attainment of this virtue. But in maximizing this one virtue, you often ignore or play down costs to other virtues, just as Plato did not seem to weigh the cruel costs his republic of perfect justice would levy on family love by first driving out everyone over ten. This is why some ideals are not only unattained but so often seem totally unattainable and, to be blunt, not worth attaining. The ideal state as portrayed by its advocates usually is not technically impossible in a narrow sense; it does not require citizens to fly to meetings with antigravity belts, or to communicate with one another by ESP, or anything like that. The ideal state is never reached in practice, and seems unreachable in any future time, because the costs of achieving it are higher than people will tolerate, and perhaps higher than they *should* tolerate. Plato's republic is chock-full of heavy costs imposed on its citizens. Although generations of his admirers have mocked people of common sense for their stolid unwillingness to live up to Plato's demands for perfection, should we not also give some credit to the person of common sense for being unwilling to shoulder costs that Plato ignored? Did Plato, I wonder, calculate how many years of perfect justice would be required to outweigh the cruelty done to those poor refugees driven from hearth and home so that the rulers could indoctrinate their children? Since he argued that even the perfect state would pass through a cycle of degeneration terminating in despotism, one cannot help wondering whether he thought that a few years of perfect justice would atone for all the injustice required to inaugurate his perfect republic. Curiously, no one seems to have asked Socrates these questions, or if they did Plato does not reveal it.

The optimal may be a good deal less dramatic than the ideal, but it does recognize that there are many important values in this world and that usually you cannot maximize one value indefinitely without creating astronomical costs to another. For instance, you can dedicate yourself completely to your private life only by having no public life, and conversely.

Because your time is valuable, you will want your association to have a system for making decisions that economizes on your time. Certainly you will not want a system that operates as if your time is of no account. Thus if you could choose between two systems for making decisions in your association that differ only in that Constitution I will require you to spend more time in decision making than Constitution II, surely you will choose Constitution II. Suppose, however, that except for the difference in time required, Constitution I is on balance better than Constitution II. Would a reasonable person opt for Constitution I? Not necessarily. You would first weigh (as best you could) the increment of value you expected from Constitution I as against the additional cost in time. The gain may or may not exceed the cost. If it does not, Constitution II may be the better.

In calculating whether Constitution I is better than Constitution II,

I need to take into account not only my own preferences for economizing on time but also the preferences of others. This has very practical consequences. Suppose that Constitution I completely accepts political equality and majority rule and lodges full sovereign authority in an assembly or town meeting. Suppose further that if I were reasonably sure that every member (or at least most members) of the association would participate actively in the assembly, I would favor Constitution I. But suppose that instead I am reasonably sure that a great many members, perhaps a majority, will not want to participate very actively and that consequently a minority of the association will be able to form a majority of the assembly. Suppose, finally, that it seems highly likely that this minority will often be unrepresentative of the views of a majority of the members. In short, Constitution I opens the way for the association to be captured and controlled by an unrepresentative minority. Since my only hope to prevent this from happening is to spend an inordinate amount of time attending meetings of the assembly and persuading others to attend meetings, and this hope is at best a slender one, I conclude that Constitution I is not optimal. Instead, I favor Constitution II, which places limits on the authority of the assembly, requires qualified majorities of two-thirds on some key issues, and compels certain matters to be approved by a referendum of all the members.

This is a rather abstract way of describing what is really a concrete problem. Let me, by way of example, draw on my own situation as a member of a university. Now it happens that my university allows a very large though not unlimited scope for decision making by the faculty. Like most of my colleagues, what attracts me to university life is primarily the opportunities it allows for doing those things that seem to me central to the purposes of a university: teaching, learning, meeting with students and colleagues in a great many informal ways, research, writing. Participating in the decisions of the university is important to me but fairly far down on the list of things I most enjoy doing or believe to be the most important objectives of a university. In short, most of us want a university to *be*. Therefore we do not want it to turn into a place where everyone spends so much time *deciding* what the university *should be* that no one has enough time to do the things that are required if a university is to *be* what it should be. I recall a colleague at a university that had been in turmoil for several years and had become highly politicized. He remarked unhappily that he could bear it when he had to attend a caucus with his allies in order to decide what position they would take in faculty meetings, but the burden really became unbearable when he had to caucus before the caucus before the meeting.

It would be out of place to burden you at this point with an optimal solution for the government of a university. The important point is that every proposed solution, and the status quo as well, should be tested not only by the criteria of Personal Choice and Competence, but also by the Criterion of Economy. Since costs must be taken into account, the optimal constitution will not only ensure that the "best" decisions are made but will also economize on time. And just as the Criterion of Competence will rule out some solutions that would be preferable by the Criterion of Personal Choice, so the Criterion of Economy will tilt the balance against some forms of university governance that might be desirable according to the other two criteria. The optimum, I suspect, will not look like anyone's ideal government. But it will be better than anyone's ideal government put into practice.

Let me round out this discussion by reminding you that even in Plato's republic the philosophers, having served full time in subordinate office between the ages of thirty-five and fifty, would thereafter make philosophy their *chief* pursuit, though "they will all take their turn at the troublesome duties of public life and act as Rulers for their country's sake, not regarding it as a distinction, but as an unavoidable task."[8] Plato does not really explain why they should not go on ruling full time, but it is clear that the idea of participating in decisions is not exactly exhilarating to the philosopher-kings. You may have forgotten that Socrates' famous parable of the cave is introduced to make the point that having come out of the cave, adjusted to the painful light of day, seen the true source of their light, the sun, and come to know that what passed for reality in the cave was mere shadows, the philosopher-guardians will not be overjoyed at the prospect of returning to the darkness and the illusions of people in the cave. And it is arguable that if the guardians did not spend more time out of the cave than in it, they would not long be competent to govern the people in the cave.

I can readily imagine objections to what I have been saying. Participation, you may say, is not quite as sharply differentiated from other activities as I have made it out to be. It is not, after all, a matter of leaving the sunlight and going back down into a dismal cave. The casual discussion at the store, on the street corner or the courthouse steps, over a meal in a college dining hall, during a stroll under the elms — all may contribute to the governing of the association. There is force in this objection. One characteristic of the small, face-to-face community as a political unit is that participation in the affairs of the association knows few sharp boundaries: the town meeting or assembly may be only the tip of the iceberg. Nonetheless, though the costs of participation may be greatly reduced in small communities, they do not vanish. The Criterion of Economy still applies. The town meeting cannot be in constant session.

You may also object that I have not made any distinction between participating in the state and in other associations. Surely the decisions of the state are so crucial that in deciding how much one should participate, personal convenience is irrelevant.

I fear that this is one of those Noble Sentiments, common in political discourse, that make us feel guilty because we cannot live up to them, make us think better of ourselves when by proclaiming them we demonstrate that our ideals are really intact after all, and befuddle the issues almost beyond hope of clarification. Let me remind you of what I said a few pages back about some of the factors that bear on the value to you of participating in the affairs of an association — in the present case, the state. To be sure, the decisions of the government of the state do quite literally deal with matters of life and death. In the importance of their consequences, direct and indirect, the decisions of the central government must surely outweigh those of any other association. What is more, the alternatives under consideration are often crucially different. Yet you must also take into account the likelihood that by increasing your participation you will change the outcome, the prospect of satisfactory outcome even if you do not participate more, and your own competence to participate more fully. I do not think a rational citizen weighing all these factors would be as little involved as are most citizens in all countries, including my own, but I suspect a reasonable upper limit for most people would fall considerably below that of the political activist.

Another and more significant consideration is that in order to participate in the affairs of a large modern state, one must participate in other associations: political parties, political movements, pressure groups, agitational groups, and the like. In the modern nation-state only an infinitesimally small percentage of citizens can participate by holding major office. The rest of us must participate in smaller associations. I need hardly remind you that the state itself is a complex entity. The United States, for example, has a national government, fifty states, and over eighty thousand local units. The national government itself is, of course, subdivided into innumerable units, as are state governments and municipalities. This multiplicity of political units imposes a heavy strain on the time of the eager citizen and demands strict application of the Criterion of Economy. A generation ago Robert Wood estimated that there were some 1,467 distinct political entities in the twenty-two-county area of the New York Metropolitan Region, "each having its own power to raise and spend the public treasure, and each operating in a jurisdiction determined more by chance than design."[9] The fifteen thousand citizens of Fridley, Minnesota, labored under eleven layers of government, each with the power to tax.[10] Obviously any effort to decide on a more desirable system of decision making for Fridley's citizens would have to give great weight to the Criterion of Economy.

Indeed one of the most forceful arguments for reducing the number of political units you must deal with is to economize on your time, attention, and energy. Yet the shape of the world we live in rules out the possibility that any single unit will be desirable. The commune, neighborhood, city-state, region, nation-state—none can possibly be, by itself, a satisfactory basis for authority.

Nor are these "political" units the only associations in which one may want to participate. I have mentioned the example of the university. It is obvious to me that I could not participate adequately in governing the university, engage actively in the decisions of all the political units that affect the quality of my life, and have any time at all for my students, let alone for writing this short book.

Let me summarize very briefly. Although the Criterion of Economy seems never to have found a prominent place in classical political theory and lacks the allure of the other criteria, it is nonetheless a criterion that a reasonable person will apply to any system of authority. In actual practice, everyone does, whether it is the Athenians delegating authority to the boulê and prytany, the New England town to the clerk and selectmen, or Tom Paine supporting representative democracy. One important resource to economize is time. A system that squanders time is, other things being equal, inferior to one that conserves it. What is more, a system of decision making that is the best according to the criteria of Personal Choice and Competence may be the worst according to the Criterion of Economy. Because what is portrayed as an ideal system of authority generally ignores certain costs, of which time is one, the "ideal" is rarely optimal. In this case, it is more rational to choose the optimal than the "ideal."

CONCLUSIONS

It has become clear by now, I hope, that the application of these three criteria requires one to judge each case on its peculiar merits. The most desirable system of authority in a particular association being what is optimal according to all three criteria, you must trade off advantages and disadvantages, costs and benefits, gains and losses. This process, alas, is rarely simple. If it were simple, one would be hard put to explain why the world's greatest political philosophers, who have wrestled with the problem of authority for several millennia, have invariably found it complex.

However that may be, the conclusion that simplistic, one-dimensional ideas about authority are bound to be wrong is an idea so threatening to those who hold simplistic one-dimensional views of the world—and their name is legion—that I fear they may reject all I have said without reflection. Yet I hope they may pause long enough to consider the possibility, which I believe to be a fact, that simple conceptions of authority are more likely to lead to despotism than to liberty, equality, and democracy or, for that matter, to a well-ordered government of wise and virtuous guardians.

It should also be clear by now that the application of our three criteria may lead you to choose political equality and majority rule in one association but not in another. The more insignificant the differences in competence on the crucial questions that fall within the scope of a particular association, the better the case for political equality among the members. And the greater the agreement among them, the stronger the case for majority rule. The case for democracy in the form of political equality and majority rule is therefore strongest where competence in the affairs of the association is widely diffused among the members and where they share a substantial consensus on all important matters. Conversely, the greater the differences in competence among the members, the weaker the case for political equality; the greater the amount of disagreement among members, the weaker the case for majority rule.

In an association where members are competent but greatly in conflict, it may make sense to dissolve the association into more harmonious groups that will be able to honor political equality and majority rule. But this solution rarely is completely attainable. For a broader association (which may be that peculiarly important association known as the state) may be necessary to regulate conflict among the smaller, more homogeneous associations. For the state and other regulatory associations, then, one may reasonably opt for political equality and at the same time a system of Mutual Guarantees that limit what simple majorities, or even any coalition short of unanimity, can do.

Thus democracy in the sense of political equality and majority rule is by no means the most desirable, that is, optimal, solution for all kinds of associations. In the extreme case, in an association where members differ crucially in their competence, such as a hospital or a passenger ship, a reasonable person will want the most competent people to have authority over the matters on which they are most competent. But if democracy is not always the most desirable basis for authority, neither are any of the alternatives to it. I have already indicated why I think aristocracy has lethal defects in the domain of the state; its disadvantages often make it inapplicable in other associations as well. Nor is any other form of authority always the most desirable. It might be a useful academic exercise to catalog all the main forms of authority and to show the advantages and defects of each. Although that tedious enterprise would serve no good purpose here, it would surely demonstrate two conclusions: that no single form of authority is the most desirable in all associations and that the possible combinations of the various forms in any concrete association must be nearly endless. Consequently, it would be folly to think that a single mass-produced model stamped out according to eternal patterns can possibly fit all the kinds of associations we need in order to cope with our extraordinarily complex world.

CHAPTER TWO

VARIETIES OF DEMOCRATIC AUTHORITY

Although democracy may not be the only acceptable form of decision making, it is one of the most important, if only because (I have argued) it is the best form for that most powerful of associations, the state.

Even democracy is not, in a strict sense, a single form of authority: it is itself an array of possibilities. Let me approach the task of clarifying what some of these possibilities are by first calling your attention to a curiously neglected and yet absolutely crucial problem: if we agree that by democracy we mean in some sense "rule by the people," we need to clarify not only what we mean by "rule" but also—and this is the aspect most often overlooked—what we mean by "the people." For by the way in which we define "the people" we shall automatically determine the way in which they can "rule"; and by the way in which we define "rule" we shall necessarily set some bounds on how "the people" can be constituted. If you are a bit mystified by these observations, it is only fair that you should be. Having puzzled over the problem for years, with astonishingly little help from the legacy of great writings about democracy, I have become persuaded that there is no theoretical solution to the puzzle, but only pragmatic ones. Meanwhile, however, it has been borne in on me that practically all the attention has been paid to the first part of "rule by the people," that is, the meaning of "rule," and almost none to the second, the meaning of "the people." All this will grow clearer as we proceed.

"The people" are those who are entitled to participate in governing: are those who are entitled to participate "the people"? There is a risk of circularity here. To break out of the circle, let me formulate the question this way: who should be entitled to participate in the government of a democratic association?

Please take very careful notice that I do not mean to raise the familiar question of *which* people among the "members" or "citizens" should be allowed to participate in governing. Even in a democratic polity some "citizens" may be excluded from political participation on grounds of competence: there is a minimum age for voting, criminals and the insane are generally excluded, and so on. No, the problem I have in mind is more fundamental and more elusive. Let me try to make clear what it is.

When we talk about raising or lowering the voting age or granting the suffrage to women, doubtless we already have in mind a specific "people," a body of "citizens" that has already defined itself as an entity: the French, the Danes, and the Dutch. Why should we take it for granted that the French, the Danes, and the Dutch are each "a people" entitled to govern themselves and not, for example, one people entitled to govern itself? The Danes do not allow the French to vote in their elections and conversely. Well, why not?

Strange as it may seem to you, how to decide who legitimately make up "the people" — or rather *a* people — and hence are entitled to govern themselves in their *own* association is a problem almost totally neglected by all the great political philosophers who write about democracy. I think this is because they take for granted that a people has already constituted itself. How a people accomplishes this mysterious transformation is therefore treated as a purely hypothetical event that has already occurred in prehistory or in a state of nature. The polis is what it is; the nation-state is what history has made it. Athenians are Athenians, Corinthians are Corinthians, and Greeks are Greeks.

If political philosophers have taken the answer for granted, you may think it foolhardy to pose the question. Let sleeping dogs lie. I ask it not only because what is taken for granted invariably conceals a question worth exploring but also because the question points to an urgent, concrete, and even contemporary problem. Are the people of Canada "a people"? Some Canadians greatly doubt it, notably many French-speaking citizens of Quebec. Are the Lithuanians a people entitled to govern themselves as an independent country? Evidently they believe so. Controversies over what particular aggregate of human beings properly constitutes "a people" for political purposes constantly surface here and there all over the globe: in the Soviet Union, North Ireland, Lebanon, Sri Lanka, among Israelis and Palestinians (and among Israelis themselves), Punjabis and other Indians, Muslims in Mindanao and other Filipinos, and so on.

The English are English, we know, and Americans are Americans. Yet when certain English people decided they were Americans there was a bloody revolution; and when certain Americans preferred a Confederacy of southerners to a Union of northerners, a devastating civil war broke out. Secession is an effort to reconstitute *the* people into *two* peoples. *If* the South had been a democracy and *if* it had managed to secede, there would have been two democracies where there had been one. The Union would have failed, but would democracy have been any worse off? Before jumping to the accepted school solution, remember that Europe consists of people who have been constituted by divisions and separations.

So long as everyone agrees that these people are Athenians and those people are Corinthians, then to advocate democracy presumably means that the citizens of Athens should govern Athens and the citizens of Corinth should govern Corinth. But suppose someone were to insist that neither the Athenians nor the Corinthians are a people but only parts of a people, that is, the Greeks. To advocate democracy would then mean, we suppose, that the citizens of Greece should govern Greece. Suppose further that a fifth-century Athenian were to insist (and if he were a fifth-century Athenian he *would* insist) that the Greeks are not *a* people but many peoples, and, therefore, each of these peoples must have its own polis and, if it chooses, its own democracy. More often than not these debates are settled by force and ratified by history: the philosophers take up where history leaves off. Is there then no rational basis for deciding what should constitute a people for purposes of democratic rule?

Or, if you prefer, who is entitled to participate in a democratic association?

Notice that you do not solve the problem by simply displacing it from the smaller entity, Athens, to the larger entity, Greece. If the Greeks took utterly for granted that the proper state was a city-state, we take it utterly for granted that the proper state is a nation-state. But if the Athenians are not a people, why are the Greeks? The question still remains unanswered.

It would occur to any American, I imagine, to say that the Greeks could have avoided their dilemma and might even have saved themselves from outside domination if they had joined together in a union that would have allowed democracy at both the "local level," as we say today, and the "national level." Athens, after all, might have yielded up some autonomy to a government of Greece and still remained "democratic." This view was so completely alien to the Greek democrat and is so completely natural to the modern democrat that if they meet in heaven they are sure to be expelled for quarreling. Moreover, the modern view still leaves the basic question unanswered, for like the other it takes for granted that what *is*, is. Since New York is a city, the people of New York should govern the city; since the United States is a nation, the people of the United States should govern the nation. But note: if the United States are still united, that is because of force and history. If the possibility of coming up with the wrong answer makes it painful for you to ask yourself on what grounds you think the people of this country are *a* people (and not several peoples), you may find it easier to ask yourself what makes New York City *a* city. But you will not, I think, find the answer any easier. After all, until 1874 New York City was only Manhattan; the present five boroughs were not consolidated until 1897; at that time Brooklyn was the fourth largest city in the country and had been an incorporated separate city since 1834. Why not reverse the process of consolidation and turn New York into five cities? or for that matter, a hundred? Or why not repeat the process and consolidate the whole metropolitan area into a single giant city, or, better, the fifty-first state? If these questions can be asked about New York, they can be asked about any existing territorial entity whatsoever, including the United States.

No matter how we might answer the question in a specific case, it seems clear that we are bound to end up with several territorial governments superimposed on one another. We may not end up with eleven units like the citizens of Fridley, but it is inconceivable that we shall end up with only one. Perhaps more than anything else this simple fact makes it inevitable that "democracy" cannot be a single form of authority but a multiplicity of forms. This crucial point will dominate the rest of this essay.

THE PRINCIPLE OF AFFECTED INTERESTS

If the answer to my question has so far eluded us, consider this appealing proposition:

> Everyone who is affected by the decisions of a government should have the right to participate in that government.

No taxation without representation. Let me call this the Principle of Affected Interests, since a handy label will prove useful.

The Principle of Affected Interests is very likely the best general principle of inclusion that you are likely to find. Yet it turns out to be a good deal less compelling than it looks. To begin with, we have already discovered that we shall have to reject it if there are significant differences in competence, as on a ship or in the operating room. The Criterion of Competence will assert its claims again. Nonetheless, if differences in competence are not at issue, and those who are affected are not less competent than those now entitled to participate, should they not be included?

One troublesome problem is that the set of persons who are affected often varies from one decision to another. Jones, Green, and you may be affected by decisions about schools, while it is Smith, Brown, and you who are affected by decisions about redevelopment. The logic of the Principle of Affected Interests is that for every different set of persons affected there be a different association or decision-making unit. To some extent this is what tends to happen, and this tendency helps explain why there were 1,467 distinct political entities in the New York Metropolitan Region and why the citizens of Fridley, Minnesota, labored beneath eleven different layers of government. The Criterion of Economy obviously argues against excessive proliferation, for how is the citizen who is affected by so many different units of government, each with its own procedures and officials, to devote much time and energy to any of them?

In the second place, the people affected by a decision are by no means affected *equally*. Consider taxes. Since I write in a country that began its rebellion against existing authority over a tax that increased the burden of Americans from an almost unnoticeable one shilling or less per person per year (compared with twenty-six shillings in Britain) to two, presumably I need not labor the point that every taxpayer is affected by taxes.[1] Since expenditures affect taxes, it is reasonable to demand "No expenditures without representation." So: let us now apply the Principle of Affected Interests. Because some public schools in California receive federal funds (my taxes), I should be entitled to vote in elections for their school boards, though my residence is some three thousand miles away. Both the Criterion of Competence and the Criterion of Economy argue strongly against this degree of direct participation; they argue instead in favor of indirect participation (which is mighty attenuated) through congressional elections, authorizations, and appropriations.

You will notice, incidentally, that the Criterion of Competence, which I had put to one side in order to examine the Principle of Affected Interests, immediately thrusts itself back into the discussion in a particularly troublesome way. Although we may agree that I am too remote (and hence incompetent) to intervene intelligently in school board elections in California, what about mayoralty elections in the city next door to me in Connecticut, New Haven? Or for that matter, New York City, particularly since as a regular reader of the *New York Times* I find myself in a captive audience for articles about politics in that city?

The ambiguity of our principle is even further increased, alas, by another consideration: what affects my interests depends on subjective factors. Is it to my interest to lower the high rate of infant mortality among residents of inner cities? reduce poverty in Appalachia? Certainly so, for my "interests" are determined by my beliefs and values about the well-being of others, like the groups just named. Notice, however, how this subjective approach enlarges one's interests and hence the possibility of being affected by the decisions of others. Notice, too, the impact of communications. The more global the network of communications that you are plugged into, the more your "interests" are likely to expand. You turn out to have an interest in the lives of rural villagers in El Salvador or India. Must you then participate in village decisions? The temptation is to practice altruistic imperialism and thus become the busybody of the world. It seems obvious that the Principle of Affected Interests must be curbed by the criteria of Competence and Economy.

If the Principle of Affected Interests, which at first glance looked as bright and clear as Sirius on a winter's night, has turned out to be a diffuse galaxy of uncountable possibilities, it is, nonetheless, not such a bad principle to start with. It gives people who believe themselves to be seriously affected by decisions at least a prima facie case for participating in those decisions and puts the burden of exclusion on those who wish to press the criteria of Competence and Economy against their claims.

By now you may be troubled by the thought that the principle has unlocked Pandora's box. Very likely it has. For example, it forces us to ask whether there is not after all some wisdom in the half-serious comment of a friend in Latin America who said that his people should be allowed to participate in our elections, for what happens in the politics of the United States is bound to have profound consequences for his country. Do not dismiss his jest as an absurdity. In a world where we all have a joint interest in survival, the real absurdity is the absence of any system of government where that joint interest is effectively represented.

FORMS OF DEMOCRACY

The prey we have been stalking is the proposition that democratic authority requires a variety of forms. The democratic idea is too grand to be trivialized by restricting itself to only one form of authority.

What many people would regard as the most perfect form of democracy, I imagine, exists within a given set of persons when every person in that set has a full and equal opportunity to participate in all decisions and in all the processes of influence, persuasion, and discussion that bear on every decision. It is easy to see that this form of democracy can exist only among a very small number of people. If you have any doubts, a simple arithmetical exercise should convince you at once. Let t be the total amount of time available for participating (for discussion, for example), h the share of time available for each participant, and p the number of persons who participate. Then p equals t/h. For example, if you have six hours set aside for discussion and voting and wish to allow each participant a half hour, then not more than a dozen persons can participate in the decision.

When decision making involves discussion (as it nearly always does), time's limits are inexorable and cruel to equal participation. This is because discussion by its very nature consists of a series of sequential acts, each taking up a block of time. When one person speaks, the others must be silent and wait their turn; otherwise there can be no discussion. In this respect, discussion is radically different from certain other ways of participating in decisions, like voting, where the participants can all act more or less simultaneously. The sequential nature of discussion means that the amount of time required increases with each participant and each act of participation. The consequences are pretty formidable, for when the number of people involved goes beyond several dozen you begin to reach the limits of physical possibility. To take an absurd example: if an association were to make one decision a day, allow ten hours a day for discussion, and permitted each member just ten minutes—rather extreme assumptions, you will agree—then the association could not have more than sixty members.

Because of the inherent limitations of this form, let me call it *committee democracy*. Anyone who has had much experience with committees will agree, I think, that the optimal size for a working committee of actively participating members can hardly be more than ten or a dozen and is probably less. But if you wish to think of an upper limit four, five, even ten times larger, it will not change the basic argument.

It will have occurred to you, I am sure, that not every person who attends a discussion feels a need to speak. You often find that your position has been adequately stated, perhaps even better stated, by someone else. This is likely to happen in an association where the members know one another well, have many opportunities to talk about the problems of the association outside of meetings called for the specific purpose of discussion and decision, and where, as is usually the case, the number of different views is considerably less than the number of members. Even if there is nowhere near time enough for every citizen to speak at the ekklesia in Athens, the New England town meeting, or the assembly of citizens (*Landsgemeinde*) in a rural Swiss canton, quite possibly everyone may speak who really wants to, and so all may feel that their viewpoint has been adequately expressed. In *primary* (or *town meeting*) *democracy*, then, the citizens may have a well-justified confidence that they really do govern directly themselves, particularly because participation is not confined to the town meeting proper but is interwoven with the totality of community life.

It is hard to say what the practical limits of primary democracy are. I recall one town meeting with nearly a thousand citizens, and once I found myself presiding over an assembly of some twenty-five hundred faculty and students. In both cases, after about four hours of debate, practically everyone who was present felt, I believe, that his or her viewpoint had been fairly presented. The issues, however, happened to have been sharply polarizing, so that the number of different positions was pretty small. You may be surprised to learn that in the age of Pericles perhaps as many as forty thousand male citizens (the exact figure is unknown) were entitled to attend the meetings of the ekklesia. In fact, however, there was not room enough for so many people to gather at the meeting place, and the evidence is pretty strong that only a small minority of the citizen body ever went to the meetings. Even so, the Assembly was not immune to the psychology of crowds, and under the influence of skillful orators it sometimes made terrible blunders.[2] But since the orators could probably have gotten themselves elected, one cannot be confident that an assembly of elected representatives would have done any better. Athens was the largest city in Greece, one of only three with more than twenty thousand citizens (the other two were in Sicily). Paradoxically, during the Golden Age of Periclean democracy, the city had probably gone beyond the limits of town meeting democracy.

My own experience leads me to believe that an assembly of one thousand people is probably too large not only because of the difficulty of ensuring that everyone can speak but also because increasing quantity means decreasing quality as the arts of rhetoric and crowd manipulation take over. It is significant that in the modern world, six hundred seems to be about the limit for legislative bodies. Taking the figure of one thousand adult citizens, men and women, would imply a total community of less than two thousand people. In practice, New England towns can, like Athens, grow much larger than this before they abandon the town meeting. My own town has a population of twenty thousand; it is the largest in Connecticut to retain some of the old town meeting system. We could debate where a reasonable upper limit might be, but I doubt whether anyone would seriously contend that primary democracy would be satisfactory if twenty thousand people regularly showed up for meetings. Again, consider the arithmetic. Allowing two minutes for each speaker in a meeting lasting six hours, less than 1 percent of the citizens would have an opportunity to speak. The larger the number of citizens, the less the chance that every citizen with a different viewpoint would be given the opportunity to present his or her views. Thus the greater the numbers, the more the town meeting runs the risk of becoming unrepresentative. This risk can be reduced only by adopting a less adventitious system of representation: choosing speakers by lot, for example, or canvassing all the positions in advance and making sure that there is a speaker for each. Or by electing representatives. These solutions, however, transform primary democracy into *representative democracy*.

Before turning to representative democracy, let me mention an intermediate possibility. An association in which the number of members is too large for primary democracy might nonetheless try to keep the decisions directly in the hands of the members in the following way. A specified number of members would be entitled to present a proposal to all the members of the association, who would then vote upon it (and upon any other alternatives presented) in an election. This is *referendum democracy*. Unlike primary democracy, and like representative democracy, referendum democracy is not limited by the size of the association. Although it does not exist as an exclusive form of decision making in the government of any country (or, so far as I know, any smaller territorial unit) it has been used for well over a century in Switzerland and the United States. In Switzerland and in most of the American states, all constitutional amendments must be submitted to a referendum. Although the procedural limitations vary a good deal, citizens may also initiate proposals for constitutional revision. As to ordinary legislation, in Switzerland citizens may insist that legislation voted on by the Federal Assembly be submitted to a referendum. In some American states, citizens may actually initiate legislation. In principle, then, the whole process of legislation could be in the hands of the citizens.

Not many countries have followed the lead of Switzerland and the United States in introducing referendum democracy, partly because experience in these two countries and elsewhere demonstrates some pretty visible limits. Just as citizens cannot be kept in constant attendance at assemblies, they often find referenda too confusing or irrelevant to sustain their interest; those who bother to vote in referenda are often only a tiny minority. Highly technical questions seem particularly unsuitable to referenda. Because of the smaller numbers who vote and bewilderment over the issues, manipulative leaders may actually be more influential in referenda than in primary democracy or representative groups. And as a practical matter, only a very small proportion of the public business can be done by means of referenda.

The occupation of the legislator is more and more approaching a full-time job.

If it is difficult to see how referendum democracy could ever be a satisfactory alternative to representative democracy, referenda can supplement representation. And in one sense referendum democracy is an integral part of representative democracy, for elections are really a form of referendum democracy. Thus representative democracy might be thought of as a system that combines referendum democracy in elections with primary and committee democracy in the legislature. I speak, of course, of the ideal, which I need not remind you is a considerable distance removed from practice.

Representative democracy carries with it certain features that make it radically different from committee democracy and even from primary and referendum democracy. Perhaps the most visible difference is in the location of authority to decide among the alternatives before the group, for where in the committee that authority is directly in the hands of the members, in representative democracy there is a two-stage process of decision making in which, as we all know, the voters choose representatives (the referendum) who are authorized to decide policy (in a primary assembly). In principle the town meeting is like the committee; in practice, as we have seen, some matters are usually delegated to representatives, such as the boulê and prytany in Athens or the town clerk and selectmen in New England.

The addition of a crucial second tier of decision making, the body of elected representatives, inevitably brings other differences. Take participation. In committee democracy, every member can participate fully in every phase of the decision; although only some are likely to speak in the town meeting, every member can attend, listen, and participate in the voting. In a representative democracy, however, although all citizens can participate in the election of representatives, only a small proportion can participate directly in making laws and policies.

One of the most important features of representative democracy in the government of the state is the appearance of political parties. These are so familiar to us that it is difficult to grasp how radical an innovation they were; in fact, it is only in the past century that democratic theory has begun to catch up with this modern institution. Even if the city-states were often riven by factionalism, in the primary democracy of the city-states political parties as we know them existed neither in theory nor in practice. Yet political parties invariably accompany the attempt to introduce representative democracy into the government of the state.

It is not going too far to say that representative democracy in the state makes political parties possible, advantageous, and inevitable. Parties are possible because the liberties entailed in representative democracy itself make them lawful: you could not suppress political parties without suppressing fundamental liberties—speech, assembly, organization, and so forth. Parties are advantageous for mobilizing voters in the election of representatives and for mobilizing representatives in the legislative body. Parties are inevitable because, being possible, once aspirants for elective office discover their advantages (as Jefferson did before and during his presidency), they will create them if they do not already exist and perpetuate them if they do. If parties begin as efficient organizations for winning votes in elections, the representatives soon press them into service for winning votes in the legislature; and if parties begin as efficient organizations for winning votes in the legislature, the representatives soon press them into service for winning votes in elections. Once one representative has a party, his opponents must. So great are the political advantages of a party that in a representative democracy a politician without a party is a politician without power.

Although possible, the political party is neither necessary nor inevitable in the committee or town meeting. Indeed, committee democracy is, typically, hostile to partisanship, for the committee reflects the familiar psychological needs of small and intimate groups. Committee members may begin as strangers but they are soon acquaintances and, in time, often friends. If they endure, committees develop a common set of standards and viewpoints that members are expected to adhere to; there are subtle (or not so subtle) punishments for those who do not. Within the intimate atmosphere of the committee, severe conflict is painful. As a result, committee members usually try to keep down conflict. Committee democracy is typically, then, consensual democracy. The members strive for unanimity, particularly on important questions. They do not try to crush an opponent; they try instead to win her over. Thus the unspoken principle of committee democracy is unanimity, not majority rule.

The town meeting is more likely than the committee to be divided into factions but less likely than the body of representatives to be divided into parties. Among friends and neighbors, party is a divisive influence. A general tendency is everywhere visible: the smaller the community, the weaker the organization of party and the more one-sided the community is in its loyalty to a party.

If they are less congenial to the growth of parties than representative democracy, the committee, the town meeting, and often the referendum may nonetheless discover parties in their midst. Wherever the committee, town meeting, or referendum are constituent elements in a larger system of representative democracy, the parties that are inevitably spawned by representative democracy are likely to intrude themselves into the activities of these smaller or alternative units.

Committee democracy, primary democracy, and representative democracy differ also in the opportunities they provide for the amateur and the professional. Although the differences are matters of degree, as you move from committee to primary to representative democracy there is a general tendency for the amateur to be increasingly displaced by the professional. Or to put the same thing in another way, the distinctions between leaders and nonleaders become sharper as leadership more and more falls to the minority who assiduously master the game of politics, invest practically all their time in political activity, and look upon political life as a vocation rather than an avocation. Professionalization and the displacement of the amateur follow from delegation and representation, for delegates and representatives are usually required to spend more time in their political roles. Once professionalism begins to appear, it is amplified by self-selection as some people choose politics for a career, while others do not.

Committee democracy, primary democracy, referendum democracy, and representative democracy are, then, radically different in form, feeling, operation, ambiance. Their differences make some people passionately prefer one to the other, even extol one and detest another. It is not difficult to understand why the Greek democrats thought there could be no democracy other than primary democracy, nor why Rousseau agreed. Yet as I hope to show in a moment, to hold that one of these forms of democracy is intrinsically better than another is nonsense.

In addition to these four forms of democracy there is a fifth form of authority (or rather a large and heterogeneous category of forms) that must be employed by all democratic states and most democratic associations and gains its legitimacy because it is a necessary instrument by which the people may rule—and yet may not be democratic in any accepted sense. I have in mind various forms of *delegated authority* that are necessary to "rule by the people," instruments, if you will, of majorities.

For example: a committee delegates the execution of a task to a particular member. The town meeting delegates authority to the town clerk and selectmen; the selectmen appoint police commissioners, who hire a constable. In Athens, remember, there was the boulê and the prytany, not to mention the juries and the elected generals. In a representative democracy the representatives are, in an abstract but important sense, delegated authorities, for the electorate delegates some (but not all) of its authority to its representative body. In turn, the representatives will almost certainly delegate authority to other officials. The criteria of Personal Choice, Competence, and Economy point so obviously to the desirability, indeed the virtual necessity, of a democratic body delegating authority to others that it seems superfluous to spell out the argument.

In a democratic association, whether governed by committee, town meeting, referendum, or representative body, the authority of delegates, agents, or subordinates is legitimate simply because (and only to the extent that) they carry out the policies of their superior, that is, the democratic body. All this is pretty familiar doctrine, I imagine. Nonetheless, this familiar doctrine leads to the paradox that democratic authority may require delegated authorities that are not, strictly speaking, democratic. I want to come back to this paradox in a moment.

IS THERE ONE BEST FORM?

It is practically impossible to speak of democracy without confusing the ideal forms with actually existing governments that are called democratic. It might be a good thing if we had different names to make clear when we mean to speak of the ideal form and when we mean some existing approximation to that ideal. For this reason over the years I have increasingly tended to use the term *polyarchy* to mean "representative democracy as we know it in practice," that is, systems with broad electorates, extensive opportunities to oppose the government and contest it in elections, competitive political parties, peaceful displacement of officials defeated in honestly conducted elections, and so on. Using the term *polyarchy* for systems of this kind has the advantage of keeping open the question of how closely polyarchy actually approximates representative democracy as an ideal.

It has a further advantage: one can begin to discuss intelligibly whether one polyarchy may not be *more* "democratic" than another, a way of thinking about "democracy" that opens up a whole new line of possibilities, for alas, the language of political theory will trap you into thinking in either-or terms. Like the youth picking off petals and saying, "She loves me, she loves me not," you will tend to say "this is a democratic association, this is not." Yet we know the world is not so simple. Some day, perhaps, we shall learn to think less simplistically about democracy; we shall then find it natural to rank political systems, or particular aspects of political systems, according to how near they are to some ideal standard of performance.

I mention all this so that you will clearly understand that even when I have drawn examples from actual governments to illustrate a point, I have been trying to describe ideal forms of authority as they might exist under favorable conditions.

Now the interaction of the realm of the particular ideal with the realm of experience is the realm of the optimal, that is, the best, taking into account all the gains and costs, or, if you like, taking not just one ideal into account but all our ideal aims at once. We have already seen that while a system of authority may be ideal according to one of our three criteria, it may not be optimal (and in this sense ideal) when all three criteria are taken into account.

This is also true of the five kinds of "democratic" authority just described. *Each is better than the others in some circumstances, but none is better than the others in all circumstances.* Many people will, I am sure, accept this proposition at once. If I dwell on it longer than they feel necessary, I do so only because some people vigorously reject it.

A Greek democrat in the time of Pericles would—and did. Yet the Greek view was nothing less than suicidal for rule by the people. Being unable to conceive of Greeks as a united people under a system of representative democracy, the Greeks condemned their primary democracy to inevitable extinction.

As every reader of *The Social Contract* knows, in that work Rousseau also rejected the proposition. To Rousseau, the only legitimate source of authority for the laws and government of the state was the assembly of the people—the town meeting. Although the specific form of government might vary,[3] no form of government was legitimate that did not receive its authority directly from the assembled people. Rousseau was the last great democratic philosopher to advocate primary democracy in a literal sense: to Rousseau it was impossible for "the people" to be "represented":

> The people's deputies are not, then, and cannot be their representatives, but only their agents [*commissaires*]; they can conclude nothing definitively. Every law that the people have not ratified in person is null; it is not a law. The English people think themselves free; they much deceive themselves; they are free only during the election of members of Parliament: once these are elected, the people are enslaved, they amount to nothing. (Book III, Ch. XV)

In his vision of primary democracy as the only legitimate kind of state or political body, Rousseau presents one of the most beguiling utopias since Plato's republic. That neither is achievable does not seem to detract, and may even enhance, their attractiveness. If the city-state was becoming obsolete in Plato's time, by Rousseau's it was an anachronism throughout the world. Yet if Rousseau's answer has been superseded by history, his question and his approach have not. In founding authority on personal choice, Rousseau was as modern as yesterday's existentialism; it was only in limiting the legitimacy of authority to the city-state that he locked himself into the prison of the past.

Beginning where Rousseau did, I argued earlier, one does not need to end where Rousseau did. Yet there is something undeniably captivating about his vision of simple people, friends, neighbors, fellow citizens, gathered together on the village green, settling their common affairs in wisdom and harmony: "When among the happiest people in the world you see groups of peasants settling the affairs of the State under an oak and always conducting themselves wisely, can you avoid contempt for the refinements of other nations, which make themselves illustrious and wretched with so much art and mystery?" (Book IV, Ch. I). The appeal is all but irresistible. Compared with primary democracy, what a sorry thing is polyarchy! Who has never felt a longing for a happy, harmonious, small, solidary political community?

It is inevitable, then, that the vision should constantly reappear. Perhaps its frequent reappearance is useful, for by calling into question all forms of authority other than primary democracy it compels rethinking; and, after all, a good deal of the power exercised in this world surely *is* illegitimate.

The most recent visitation of the vision was during the 1960s when it revealed itself to some elements of the New Left who, not realizing how much they were merely restating a very ancient tradition, insisted that people who are affected by decisions have the right to participate directly in making those decisions. Their demand for "participatory democracy" was simply a renewed assertion of Rousseau's insistence that the only legitimate source of authority is primary democracy. By the end of the decade the ideology of participatory democracy was rapidly waning; it was a youthful fashion of the sixties, which the youth of the eighties disdained as the foolish idea of their elders.

Yet the claim and the vision have so much moral and psychological validity that it would be a pity, I think, if these demands for primary—or participatory—democracy were to become simply another episode in the long history of failure to find viable units by which people can participate directly and effectively in shaping the decisions that affect them.

THE DILEMMA OF PRIMARY DEMOCRACY

I doubt whether any recent advocate of participatory democracy has made a case one-tenth as powerful as Rousseau made his. Let Rousseau stand, then, as the best advocate of participatory democracy we have. When you emerge from the spell cast over you by *The Social Contract*, what do you find? An argument so flawed as to be of precious little help today.

To begin with, the argument tends to distort reality by overlooking a vast body of concrete experience that shows that primary democracy, like polyarchy, is sure to witness the emergence of factions and leaders. Readers of *The Social Contract* do not learn much about factionalism and leadership in primary democracies, other than that these are evils to be avoided. Yet Rousseau should have known that they are evils that cannot be avoided. One would gather from *The Social Contract* that the city of which he was such a proud citizen was a flawless primary democracy. Yet the Republic of Geneva "was the only government in Europe to condemn *The Social Contract* at the moment of publication." Along with *Emile*, it was burned before the town hall, and Rousseau was "declared liable to arrest upon entrance into the city."[4] These illiberal acts were hardly the product of a harmonious people. They were the actions of an aristocratic body of leaders and were opposed by the burghers, who, though indignant, did nothing. Six years later, however, the burghers revolted and took power; in 1782 they in turn were thrown out in an aristocratic revolution assisted by French military forces.[5] A harmonious republic?

If Geneva were an exception, we could overlook Rousseau's patriotic astigmatism. But as the history of Greece and Italy showed,

Geneva was no exception. The facts of faction were plain enough. So plain, indeed, that a few years later during the American Constitutional Convention and in *The Federalist* James Madison took as inevitable what Rousseau took as avoidable. Madison stood *The Social Contract* on its head—deliberately, it is safe to assume. Where Rousseau seemed to hold that because factions and leadership must be avoided in the perfect state, it was therefore unnecessary to provide institutions for dealing with them, Madison evidently believed that precisely because they could not be avoided in an optimal state, it was necessary to provide institutions for dealing with them.

Rousseau's neglect is characteristic of many advocates of primary democracy. Because of this neglect, these advocates often seem either naive or Machiavellian: naive when they speak of "the people" as if the people were a single, well-defined, harmonious unit, Machiavellian when they use the rhetoric of "power to the people" to conceal their attempts to gain power for their own faction. Rousseau's neglect is also the source of the totalitarian strain that some critics have in my view attributed wrongly to him but rightly to many of his followers. From the axiom that factions and leaders are evil it is a simple step to the conclusion that they must be suppressed. Whoever announces this conclusion turns out to mean that in order for "the people" to act through their authentic agents, which are of course his own faction, all other factions and leaders must be suppressed.

A second flaw is that Rousseau provides us with no criteria for deciding what constitutes a people. Like most of his predecessors and successors, Rousseau assumes that history and prehistory take care of the problem. That "the people" must rule by assembling together and passing laws is clear enough: but what people constitute "the people"? Rousseau does not tell us. Strangely enough, he seems more content than he should be with answers that have nothing but history to make them acceptable. Although he demonstrates with his usual persuasiveness that no man can rightfully be the slave of another (Book I, Ch. IV), he does not lament the fact that along with women and foreigners, slaves were excluded from the primary democracy of Athens. Quite the contrary: thanks to the work of the slaves, "the people" could almost always be meeting in assembly (Book III, Ch. XV)! He approves of the fact that in the Roman republic, few weeks passed without an assembly of *le peuple romain* (Book III, Ch. XII); but of course only a part of the Roman populace was ever able to assemble in Rome. To Rousseau, the people consist of the citizens, and the citizens make up the people (Book I, Ch. VI); but that some people are not citizens, and hence not a part of the people, leaves Rousseau surprisingly unconcerned. Indeed, throughout his life he seems to have accepted with equanimity the fact that in his native Geneva, which he so idealized, about three-quarters of the adult population were excluded from citizenship. As in Athens and Rome, so in Rousseau's Geneva the people were greatly outnumbered by the nonpeople.[6] You might ignore these as historical blind spots if they did not so vividly make the point: Rousseau insists that the people, as citizens, are entitled to rule, but he does not tell us what people are entitled to be citizens.

Once again, he opens a flank to the charge of being potentially antidemocratic. Thus even if the Republic of Venice was governed by less than two thousand nobles, that did not mean to Rousseau that Venice was a true aristocracy, for though the people had no part in the government, the nobility itself constituted the people (Book IV, Ch. III)! The same logic was used by Americans in the antebellum South to prove that democracy flourished in the southern states: there "the people" meant white people. Bemused by the problem of what constitutes a people, even so shrewd an analyst of democratic theory as Joseph Schumpeter came to the astounding conclusion that "the rule of the Bolshevik party would not *per se* entitle us to call the Soviet Republic undemocratic. We are entitled to call it so only if the Bolshevik party itself is managed in an undemocratic manner —as it obviously is."[7] It is very hard to know where such reasoning may stop, but let me suggest what must surely approach the limit of inanity by drawing the conclusion that a country of 300 million people is governed democratically provided only that the triumvirate of dictators who rule it operate by majority rule.

Although a modern advocate of primary democracy might not fall into traps so visible to the contemporary eye, such an advocate is bound to fall into others. One cannot define "the people" without creating for oneself a dilemma on the horns of which one must ultimately be impaled.

To see why this is so, let me consider the third and most familiar flaw, which has certainly been on the reader's mind all along. Any argument that no political system is legitimate unless all the basic laws and decisions are made by the assembled people leads inexorably to the conclusion that the citizen body must be quite small in number.

So far as I know, for centuries everyone has agreed that the premises entail this conclusion. Are we then to say that, by definition, "the people" can only be a group small enough to engage in primary democracy? But if primary democracy were the only legitimate kind of political system, then no country now existing in the world, except perhaps a few island microstates, could possibly have a legitimate government.[8] This consequence is enough to boggle the mind even of one who, like me, hardly regards the nation-state as a sacred entity. Aside from the fact that no nation is likely to dissolve itself into tiny states simply and in order to create a multiplicity of primary democracies, quite obviously if it did it would be very much worse off than before with respect to a vast range of problems.

Pollution, for one. It was once reported that "the rain in some parts of Sweden is about as acid as Coca-Cola. . . . This acidity is attributed to the oxides of sulfur that belch out of England's and northern Europe's industries."[9] I could go on multiplying examples indefinitely: nuclear testing, public health, medical care, the control of economic enterprises, monetary and fiscal policies, racial discrimination, poverty, crime, access to raw materials, capital, consumers' goods, markets, military aggression, hegemony, war, and the destruction of the small state. In a world of microstates, let there arise only one large and aggressive state and the microrepublics are doomed. Either they must suffer subjugation or they must unite in mutual defense. Neither outcome will allow all important decisions to be made in primary assemblies. The force of these objections is so strong that one wonders how the advocate of primary democracy can fail to feel it. I do not myself know any answer except that the capacity of a human mind, however brilliant, to be dazzled by beautiful but insubstantial schemes has no more limits in politics than in real estate or the stock market. Rousseau himself, however, was too knowledgeable not to be aware that he was obliged to explain how his little republics were to survive: "I do not see how it would be . . . possible for the sovereign to conserve among us the exercise of its rights, if the city is not very small. But if it is very small, will it be subjugated? No" (Book III, Ch. XV). Rousseau thereupon promised his readers another work in which he would show how the fatal flaw could be eliminated. He never kept his promise. In a footnote he hinted that the solution lies in confederations, but given the principles Rousseau had so carefully laid out in *The Social Contract* I do not see how the government of a confederacy could possibly be legitimate.[10]

If a state is too small to deal effectively with certain crucial matters, then either it may be possible for the government of some larger system to be rightful or no rightful government can deal with these problems. If the first, then primary democracy cannot be the only source of authority. If the second, then we are led to the absurdity that a rightful government might be less desirable than some system of wrongful power. The absurdity should be most evident to those who insist that everyone who is affected by decisions should have the right to participate in making them. For if everyone had to participate directly, then most people whose interests are affected by decisions on matters of the kind I mentioned a moment ago could not participate at all. The remaining alternative is to say that on matters like these, most people affected by decisions will be able to participate only indirectly.

This may be a cruel choice, but I see no way of escaping it. To insist upon primary democracy as the exclusive form of democracy is to condemn "the people" to impotence. True, to the extent their larger neighbors allow, the people in a microstate can rule; but they may have very little to rule over.

THE CHINESE BOXES

I invite you now to engage in a mental experiment that I fear you may resist as preposterous. I want you to imagine that you are trying to constitute a system of rightful government for the world, a system whose laws you would ordinarily feel obliged to obey. I want you to assume further that to be rightful the system must be in some sense "democratic," that it must be designed to facilitate "rule by the people": not just a single people, now, nor *the* people as one parochial ideologue or another might define the people, but rule by the people of the world.

If you resist this exercise, remember that in their Golden Age the Greeks refused to consider seriously a constitution for the whole of Greece, tiny as that entity seems by modern standards. Remember too that as late as the eighteenth century, it was still an article of faith, which the men at the American Constitutional Convention undertook to challenge, that you could not have a republic on a territory as large as the thirteen states. In 1990 a government for the world is, I admit, a fantastic idea; it will not seem so in a century. Nor will it then seem strange to ask whether and to what extent such a government can or should be "democratic," and how it might be.

My reason for asking you to participate in this exercise is, however, not a practical one. I have purely intellectual purposes in mind. Or perhaps spiritual: I am not yet sure of having exorcised a ghost that has been haunting us.

Whenever I try to imagine what such a constitution might be, I am at once drawn to the conclusion that it must contain extensive mutual guarantees limiting the scope of the majority principle. If, as I argued earlier, the majority principle requires such a high degree of trust and consensus that majorities are almost invariably limited even within the nation-state, then surely people of different languages, races, religions, and national origins, far removed from one another in space, speech, and thought, and with no firm habits of political cooperation and mutual trust, will never voluntarily unite or remain under a single constitution unless the matters they value most are protected from invasion by majorities. Indeed, who can say what majorities and minorities would form on what issues? I do not doubt that in every country a few people of great goodwill and enormously poor judgment could be found who would support the majority principle in a world constitution; but I am quite certain that they would be swept aside by the majority of people (or other and larger minorities) in their own country.

You do not need to be told that the world could not possibly be governed by primary democracy. Assuming that the people of the world could be governed by any form of "democracy" at all, obviously they would need to delegate authority to representatives. Yet even polyarchy with two levels of authority—the people and their representatives—would be incapable of governing the world. Imagine if you can a general assembly made up of representatives elected by the people of the world. If Rousseau himself was scarcely able to conceive circumstances in which a body of people could enact laws in a primary assembly and also administer them with no delegation whatsoever, no reader, I imagine, would envision a world polyarchy without authority delegated from the representative assembly to executive and administrative agencies. So we shall have to provide for at least three levels of authority—the people, their representatives, and the administration. Suppose then that the world government were to consist *only* of the elected assembly, a cabinet directly responsible to the assembly, and administrative agencies directly responsible to the cabinet (indirectly to the assembly). No other government would exist. As with Plato's republic, what boggles the mind is how such a system could ever get started; one needs a Creator, or a Big Bang. But what is equally mind-boggling is how such a system could ever last beyond the first Monday after the Creation. It is hard for me to conceive how a "world democracy" could be made more oppressive and stultifying than by having it consist of nothing but elections and a representative body on the one side, and a cabinet and bureaucracies on the other. Let your mind play for a moment with the thought of the World Minister of Education regulating your schools and the World Minister of Urban Affairs deciding whether a highway should go through your neighborhood. By comparison, the once overcentralized bureaucracy of France would look like a miracle of efficiency.

In fact, by Tuesday the French would, I am sure, demand that the old and suddenly attractive system be restored; by Friday revolutions against central authority would spatter the globe. What new levels of authority might be added? If we assume that the Creation, or the Big Bang, had not totally eradicated all memories of the past, then for many people it would be a natural step to demand some elbow room for smaller units constituted somewhat along the boundaries of the old nation-states. To be sure, some of the countries that are now held together more by bayonets and baling wire than by common feeling would like Humpty Dumpty be too fractured for the pieces to be put together again. Yet people sharing a common territory, language, past, and fellow feeling more concrete than abstract humanity would surely demand some decentralization to a unit in which they might reasonably expect to share some aims, feelings, outlooks, and ways of doing things. If you will be patient for the sake of the experiment and let me now make the wildly improbable assumption that these units would be "democratic" (which, because of their size, means polyarchies), our world government now has an intermediate stage of "democracy" in the form of polyarchy-cum-administration.

It is easy to see that only one intermediate stage would be insufficient, for the intermediate units would be either too large or too small. Nations even as small as the Scandinavian democracies are too large to handle satisfactorily all the problems that involve local variation, such as neighborhood planning. As for giant nations, no one has ever devised a sensible scheme by which the people of the United States could govern themselves without several intermediate stages between the people and the federal government. The eleven-tier system of Fridley, Minnesota, may be an absurd proliferation; yet it is a good deal less absurd than trying to govern a world region as large as the United States with no lower levels of authority. If nations are too large for local variations, cities are too small for regional variations of the kind manageable by provinces or the nation-state.

So: you throw in another stage or two of polyarchy-cum-administration, a stage of primary democracy at the neighborhood level, a dash of committee democracy, possibly even an opportunity for referenda.

The system is getting complicated. In practice, any sensible effort to devise a scheme for world democracy would have to be very much more complex than anything we need to envision here. But our mental experiment has, I hope, already made the point I was reaching for. For two thousand years, philosophers who wrote about rule by the people took it for granted that "the people" would be a single, well-defined, and probably small subset of humanity, and that this subset of people would rule through a single, sharply bounded, and completely autonomous state. Just as the consequence of this way of thinking for the Greek democrat was to envision a map of a "democratic" Greece as all fenced off into autonomous, independent, democratic, and usually warring city-states, each totally legitimate within its own boundaries and totally illegitimate outside them, so the consequence of the ancients' way of thinking about a "democratic" world is to imagine it made up of autonomous, independent, democratic states. Within the walls of their state, the people rule. But they have no authority outside their walls, and therefore no authority for dealing with matters that transcend their boundaries, for example, pollution, nuclear testing, and violence.

I will be told that no progressive person really thinks that way these days. It is true that no progressive-minded person would *admit* to thinking in this way. The trouble is that it is difficult for one to divest oneself of ancient ways of thought so deeply embedded in our very assumptions about democracy that one is often unaware of them exactly when they most constrict the imagination. My mental experiment was an attempt to enable readers to liberate themselves from the last unconscious vestiges of that antique style of thought, for in our world it is an invitation to suicide.

The alternative way of thinking about rule by the people comes easy for people who live in federal systems, as in Australia, Canada, Switzerland, and the United States. Democratic federalist ideas take for granted that there must be several stages of "democratic" governments; that "the people" who are entitled to "rule" at one stage are a subset of "the people" who are entitled to "rule" at a more inclusive stage; and that the rights and obligations of "the people" at various stages are embodied in a system of mutual guarantees.

If you have concurred in my argument up to now, then I think you must agree with me that stages of government fitting together rather like the components of a Chinese box are necessary if "the people" are to "rule" on matters important to them, whether a neighborhood playground, water pollution, or the effective prohibition of nuclear war. From which we must conclude that whatever stages are necessary in order for "the people" to "rule" effectively on matters important to them are also, from a purely democratic point of view, rightful.

Whether you want to say that each stage is equally "democratic" is another question. I do not believe there is any contradiction in saying that in order for the people to make their choices effective on matters of importance to them they will need some stages of government that are less "democratic" than others. Earlier I referred to the need for delegated authority. A representative body, I suggested, may itself be viewed as delegated authority, but in order to be effective, representative bodies need to delegate authority still further to administrative bodies. Polyarchy-cum-administration is delegation-cum-delegation. When members of a democratic body delegate some of its authority in order to effectuate their purposes, they will want to ensure that the authority is employed for the purposes they have in mind. Delegated authority is subordinate authority. In this sense, delegated authority entails hierarchy. And the more dangerous the authority, or the more open it is to abuse, the stronger we may want the controls within hierarchy to be. If the people who constitute a city's police force were entitled to decide on the purposes for which they would use their power, then the citizens of the city—"the people"—would be unable to rule the city. The fact that this happens too much already is no reason for wanting it to happen more.

In short, if you want to maximize the effectiveness of the people in achieving their purposes, you will need some stages of government that you may consider less "democratic" than others. If you think that polyarchy is less "democratic" than primary democracy, you will nonetheless need to prescribe several stages of polyarchy. What is more, you will need administration, and administration will need hierarchy. Otherwise, "the people" who rule may turn out not to be the people but the bureaucrats. I do not see how we can stretch the meaning of "democratic" authority to include the hierarchy of administration. Consequently we must conclude that rule by the people requires not only democratic forms but also nondemocratic forms of delegated authority.

It would be dishonest and irresponsible of me to draw simple prescriptions from this analysis. The criteria of Personal Choice, Competence, and Economy cannot be applied mechanically. Alas, even the age of computers will not relieve you of hard choices and dangerous decisions.

I cannot therefore exhort you: the only rightful government is primary democracy. Or: place all your trust in polyarchy. Or: the world must be governed by a federal democracy.

Perhaps the greatest error in thinking about democratic authority is to believe that ideas about democracy and authority are simple and must lead to simple prescriptions. I hope you have seen why this cannot be so. If you do, then we could begin a dialogue on how to develop democracy and rightful authority in our world, our country, our corporations, universities, cities, neighborhoods. In the next part of this essay, I shall try to begin my part of the dialogue. But if you still think there are simple prescriptions, then we cannot hope to understand one another.

The simplest way to think about democracy is to conceive of it as a single, invariant ideal form of government. I have tried to show why rule by the people requires not one form but many forms, including, paradoxically, nondemocratic forms of delegated authority. Yet the error of thinking about democracy as a single form has led to catastrophe in the past; I fear it will lead to disaster in the future.

If the French Revolution ended in Napoleon, it was partly because the Jacobins did not wholly understand that France had to be governed by polyarchy, not by primary democracy. In opposition, and without responsibility for governing, Robespierre sympathized with ideas of primary democracy. In a nation where Rousseau was the main democratic ideologue, how could he do otherwise? But when he had the obligation to govern, naturally he rejected primary democracy. "Democracy," he said in direct contradiction to Rousseau, "is not a state in which the people, continually assembled, itself directs public affairs. . . . Democracy is a state in which the sovereign people, guided by laws of its own making, does for itself what it can do well, and by its delegates what it cannot."[11] Nonetheless, having rejected Rousseau and primary democracy he could not conceive of polyarchy, with its pluralism, factions, parties, oppositions, political competition. How could he? Unlike nature, in politics birth often precedes conception. Across the ocean polyarchy was being born; but it had not yet been conceived. Confronted with the realities of governing, the Jacobins understood that a handful of sans-culottes were not the people of Paris, and the people of Paris were not the people of France. They knew that in order for the people to rule, the people had to have representatives. But the Jacobins never understood the complexities of polyarchy. So in place of primary democracy they substituted committee democracy; but since the Committee of Public Safety did not know how to transform itself into a polyarchy it transformed itself into a dictatorship. The example of Robespierre is still emulated: dictators rule in the name of the people but provide the people with no means by which they can invalidate that claim. The dictator may be of the people, he will claim to rule for the people, but he will suppress anyone who attempts to achieve rule by the people.

To assert that democratization must always require primary democracy is a perfect strategy for preventing large numbers of people from governing themselves effectively. Yet to believe that democratization always requires polyarchy is equally fatuous. During our mental experiment a moment ago we began with an elected world parliament: polyarchy-cum-administration at the level of the world. The experiment, you remember, had to be set going by a deus ex machina. Since a "democratic" world government is unlikely to be established either by a Creator or a Big Bang, in practice it can evolve only as rapidly as countries are willing to enter into the mutual guarantees that will underpin the authority of world law. In the early stages of evolution, therefore, the institutions of world government are necessarily in the form of delegated authority, not polyarchy. To insist that no system of world government can be rightful unless it operates with the full panoply of polyarchal institutions — elections, representatives, competing parties, and the rest — means that there cannot possibly be a rightful world order in time to rescue humanity from the gradual or sudden destruction that seems so inevitable a destiny if relations among nation-states cannot be brought more effectively under the control of law. Most nation-states do not now practice polyarchy within their own boundaries. How can they possibly be expected to permit free elections for representatives to a world parliament when they do not permit free elections for representatives to a national parliament? No, if it comes in time to save us, world government will have to evolve not through polyarchy but through delegated authority.

At the other extreme, to suppose that primary democracy cannot be rightful without organized parties competing in elections and presiding over conflicts between governments and oppositions seems to me equally fatuous. Town meetings are not always harmonious, the general good is not always visible, the general will does not always emerge. Nonetheless, organized, competing, institutionalized political parties often introduce an additional element of conflict and interest that obfuscates the search for mutually satisfactory solutions.

The problem then is always to find the form most appropriate to the circumstances. Reasonable people may disagree on what is most appropriate in particular circumstances. But so long as they agree that no one form is suitable for all circumstances they stand some chance of finding a form of authority suitable for the particular circumstances.

OF HUMAN DIMENSION

Yet there is in Rousseau's vision of the small democracy a conception of human dimensions that we should not lose sight of. As the dimensions of our social universe have multiplied over the last several centuries, humanity—I use the vague collective noun thought appropriate for statements of this kind—has gained in power over the environment. Yet the mechanisms through which that control is exerted are so complex that humanity in the singular, the individual man or woman, often has little sense of control over the decisions that flow from these mechanisms. Humanity has grown vastly more powerful, but individuals feel less powerful. Even polyarchy is a democratic Leviathan, more often than not benign and decent, but like Kafka's Castle vast, remote, inaccessible.

In a difficult paragraph in *The Social Contract*, Rousseau foreshadows the democratic Leviathan and the feelings that attach to it. Suppose, he writes, that the state is composed of ten thousand citizens. The sovereign people may be thought of as a single collective body. But the particular citizen who is subject to the laws of that sovereign remains a single individual. So he may be said to have one ten-thousandth share in the sovereign authority. But if there are a hundred thousand citizens, then the share of each in the sovereign authority is only one hundred-thousandth. "Thus, the subject remaining always one, the relation of the sovereign increases in proportion to the number of citizens. From which it follows that the more the State grows, the more liberty diminishes" (Book III, Ch. I).

The exact meaning of this passage is obscure, and I have more than a sneaking suspicion that Rousseau's logic here does not stand up under close examination. What is important for our purposes is the notion that as the number of people in a democratic association increases, the smaller the share each individual must have in its decisions. The collective grows larger; the individual shrinks—in influence, power, liberty, capacity for shaping the laws to which he or she is subject.

By now it is no doubt quite clear to you how you might turn the argument upside down. To the extent that a small association cannot deal effectively with important problems that spill beyond its boundaries, then a larger association might be more effective.

Thus common sense tugs in opposite directions. One moment it seems to say: be effective—make your association small. The next it says: be effective — make your association as large as need be. The reductio ad absurdum of the first is an association of one; of the second, the whole world (now that it is reasonable to believe in life in other solar systems, shall we say the whole universe?).

What is needed to resolve the paradox is a distinction between individual effectiveness and collective effectiveness. In an association operating under democratic rules, the impact of an individual on a decision decreases with the number of citizens, whereas the effectiveness of the whole body of citizens, the collectivity, often (but by no means invariably) increases with the number of people and extent of area within its jurisdiction.

Other things being equal, you stand a better chance of affecting the outcome of an election in an association of 100 members than in one with 100 million members. The point is intuitively obvious. Although the measurement of influence is a subject bristling with difficulties and disagreements, so far as I know everyone who has systematically investigated this thorny subject agrees with common sense: in any system operating according to democratic rules, the chance that a particular voter can affect the outcome of an election, referendum, or other voting decision must necessarily diminish as the number of voters increases. In this respect, Rousseau was right.

But other things are *not* equal, and in this respect Rousseau was wrong. Unless you have completely lost the point of voting, you are not interested in the outcome of voting per se, for taken strictly by itself voting is no more than a kind of opinion poll. What makes voting different from — and generally more important than — an opinion poll is that it is instrumental to other objectives. The outcome of the voting has consequences; it is the consequences you are mainly interested in. It follows then that you will want to consider your influence, impact, or effectiveness as a function not only of the effect of your vote on the outcome of the election but also of the value, weight, or importance of the consequences of the outcome. As a function of the effect of your vote on the outcome of the election, your effectiveness necessarily decreases with the number of voters, but as a function of the value of the consequences, your effectiveness often increases with the size of the association, for the larger association can often cope with certain matters more effectively than the smaller association. In which are you potentially most effective in liberating yourself from upstream pollution of your water supply: an association with 10,000 members and no jurisdiction over the polluters or an association with 100,000 members, including the polluters? To exist without being poisoned is, surely, a rather basic liberty. If to guarantee that liberty requires the larger association, does it make sense to say that you must necessarily have less liberty in the large association?

I suppose all this is perfectly obvious. Yet it is a fact that intelligent people do get trapped by the kind of reasoning employed by Rousseau, even if they have never read Rousseau.

Must we conclude that an association should be enlarged in every case where it can be shown that by doing so, some matter like pollution can be dealt with more effectively in the larger than in the smaller association? Clearly not. In the first place, we must not relapse into a way of thinking from which I have tried to liberate you: that there must be only a single, all-purpose association, the one sovereign state. Let me remind you again of the now familiar point: we need associations of different dimensions, for different purposes.

In the second place, since you cannot possibly keep a large number of associations at the focus of your attention, energy, and action, it would be foolish to proliferate associations for every problem (as Americans have a tendency to do). As a practical matter you will have to put some things into your Chinese boxes that do not quite fit, on the ground that the advantages of fewer boxes will outweigh the disadvantages of the inexact fit, at least up to some point that I fear can only be satisfactorily defined in practice.

In the third place, it is crucially important to keep in mind that the extra costs imposed by large organizations are often enormous. That they can bring a matter more fully within their jurisdiction than a smaller organization does not always mean, of course, that they can deal with it effectively. But even if they can, the costs may exceed the gains. Among the costs are the creation of an individual sense of impotence that can be demoralizing and dehumanizing: a feeling that decisions are beyond your control, that your own small voice can never be heard amid the din of a million or a hundred million others, that to the decision makers of the world, engaged today in a lazy game of Indian wrestling and tomorrow, knives drawn, in a struggle to the death, you are as an ant scurrying underfoot, your fate dependent on nothing more than where these giants happen to thrust a foot or crash awkwardly to earth.

It would be comforting to have a crystal-clear rule of action, the kind of rule theorists adore and decision makers disdain. Although I recommend that you deny yourself the dangerous comforts of simplistic thinking, the argument does suggest a few pragmatic principles:

1. If a matter is best dealt with by a democratic association, seek always to have that matter dealt with by the smallest association that can deal with it satisfactorily.

2. In considering whether a larger association would be more satisfactory, do not fail to consider its extra costs, including a possible increase in the sense of individual powerlessness.

3. The Criterion of Economy requires that the number of democratic associations in which you participate are few, even if this means that all are too large or too small for some matters.

4. Remember that the alternatives to a larger association include not only a smaller association but also Autonomous Decisions—for example, Consumers' Choice through the market, and so forth.

CHAPTER THREE

DEMOCRACY AND

MARKETS

I t is a historical fact that modern democratic institutions (that is, actually existing though not ideal democracy) have existed only in countries with predominantly privately owned, market-oriented economies, or capitalism if you prefer that name. It is also a historical fact that all "socialist" countries with predominantly state-owned, centrally directed economic orders—command economies—have not enjoyed democratic governments but have in fact been ruled by authoritarian dictatorships. It is also a historical fact that some "capitalist" countries have also been—and are—ruled by authoritarian dictatorships.

To put it more formally, it looks to be the case that market-oriented economies are necessary to democratic institutions, though they are certainly not sufficient. And it looks to be the case that state-owned, centrally directed economic orders are strictly associated with authoritarian regimes, though authoritarianism definitely does not require them. We have something very much like a historical experiment, so it would appear, that leaves these conclusions in no great doubt.

Of course, there is an enormous amount of complexity, variation, and qualification packed into my all-too-brief description of the experiment and the conclusions from it. Only metaphorically is history a laboratory; we cannot rerun the experiment at will to sort out all the causal factors. Thus the apparently strict association between dictatorship and the state-owned, centrally directed economic orders

This chapter is adapted from "Social Reality and 'Free Markets': A Letter to Friends in Eastern Europe," *Dissent* (Spring 1990): 224–28.

of the "socialist" countries is contaminated, so to speak, by Leninism. With its arrogant assignment of the role of vanguard to the Communist party, which in practice means the hegemony of the party leaders (or leader) in a one-party system, orthodox Leninism denies a place to the political pluralism that a country requires if it is to be democratic. Even during the brief period of the New Economic Policy, Leninist doctrine led directly to the suppression of opposition parties. In short, independently of a state-owned, centrally directed economy, Leninist political views would no doubt have been sufficient to bring about the suppression of oppositions and the creation of authoritarian regimes.

If the historical experiment is not as clear-cut as it looks, there are nonetheless good reasons for thinking that a predominantly state-owned, centrally directed economy will prove to be incompatible with democracy in the not-so-long run. Such an economic order places enormous resources in the hands of leaders—resources for persuasion, inducement, corruption, and coercion. As far as I know, the only instances in democratic countries of a centrally directed economy (though not widespread state ownership) were the comparatively brief experiences of Britain and the United States in the Second World War, when the need to mobilize all possible resources for the war effort led to the creation of systems of centralized allocations and price fixing. Although these systems performed magnificently in achieving their limited purposes, in both countries they were rapidly dismantled after the war ended—in part because the public would no longer tolerate the restrictions they imposed. Had they endured, I shudder to think of the effects they could have had on American and British political life. In the United States, even a scrupulous president would have found it hard to resist the temptation to use his power over the economy to discourage opposition. An unscrupulous president—Richard Nixon comes immediately to mind—might well have used that power in far more sinister ways.

Therefore, even if systems of state ownership and centralized direction of the economy had not proved themselves inefficient in meeting the needs of relatively modern well-developed countries—as they clearly have—we would be wise to reject them on the separate ground that they pose a standing danger to democratic institutions. Nevertheless, I want to suggest that our path lies somewhere between full reliance on a market economy and the excessively centralized economic system that, as I write, the people of the Soviet Union and Eastern Europe are rightly rejecting.

In urging these considerations, I am reminded of a book published nearly half a century ago that bears rereading today—*The Great Transformation* by Karl Polanyi.[1] Polanyi argued that the visible failures of state intervention in England from the 1790s to the 1830s, particularly the disastrous consequences of the Poor Laws, profoundly influenced the theories of several generations of important thinkers, from Bentham, Burke, and Malthus to Ricardo, Marx, Mill, Darwin, and Spencer. The lesson many liberal thinkers of the time drew was that state intervention, even for humane ends like the care of the rural poor, was likely to cause far more harm than good. The alternative they should support instead, they concluded, was a full market economy with self-regulating markets in land, labor, capital, and money. And with the passage of Poor Law Reform in 1834, a self-regulating market economy seemed finally to have arrived.

Yet no sooner had it arrived than discontent with its consequences began to bring about state intervention to regulate markets—efforts so successful that Herbert Spencer, an advocate of unregulated market capitalism, lamented the long list of regulatory actions he could compile by 1884: regulations governing food and drink, penalizing the employment in mines of boys under twelve not attending schools and unable to read and write, empowering Poor Law officials to enforce vaccination, extending compulsory vaccination to Scotland and Ireland, punishing chimney sweepers who compelled boys to sweep chimneys so narrow that the boys often suffered injuries and sometimes death, providing controls for contagious diseases, empowering local officials to set up public libraries at public expense . . . the list went on for several pages. And since 1884 the list has lengthened. Even in the United States, which is often thought of as the very citadel of laissez-faire capitalism, to describe briefly all the ways in which governments—national, state, municipal, regional, district, and so on—regulate, supplement, displace, or otherwise alter the operation of markets would take a small library.

Polanyi's account is consistent with a much broader range of historical experiences in the countries where today we find not only the most stable and long-lived democratic systems but also the most advanced and successful market economies, in Europe, North America, and the Pacific. From the experiences of these countries we can, I think, draw the following conclusions.

1. **Many of the criticisms of capitalism advanced by socialists were essentially correct.** Capitalism is persistently at odds with values of equity, fairness, political equality among all citizens, and democracy. Where many socialists went badly wrong was in believing that the evils they saw could best be solved by abolishing markets, competition among economic enterprises, and the seeming anarchy of the price system, and transferring the ownership and direct control of the economy to "the public" or "society," as represented by the state. In Western Europe, however, socialists discovered that they could not achieve these goals; they were unable to replace capitalism with the centralized state socialism many of them believed to be ideally preferable; and they turned their political efforts instead to finding specific solutions to the concrete problems that a market economy inevitably gives rise to. Thus though they never achieved "socialism" as they commonly thought of it, they did help to make their economies more decent, humane, and just than was the capitalism of Marx's time.

2. **In doing so, socialist, labor, and social democratic parties contributed to—though they were not the sole authors of—the development of the mixed economies that exist in advanced countries today.** If these mixed economies are a far cry from the centralized systems that were created in Eastern Europe under Leninist rulers, they are also very far from the classical liberal model of a self-regulating market economy. If we look to the most advanced economies for guidance, then we should not allow ourselves to be misled by dogma about "free markets." Although the economies of these countries are often described as "free market" systems, they are not. Instead, all the world's most advanced and successful econ-

omies are mixtures of markets (themselves of enormous variety) and deliberately imposed government interventions in the market (also of incredible variety).

3. In addition, a century or more of efforts to arrive at a feasible and politically acceptable mix of market and nonmarket elements has not produced a definitive, stable, or uniform solution. There is not the slightest reason to think that the search for the best mix has anywhere come to an end. The United States, for example, harvested the consequences of eight years of the Reagan administration during which deregulation and worship of the beneficent effects of the market dominated the thinking, and to some extent the policies, of that administration. In the post-Reagan years, Americans began to discover—or rather rediscover—how much damage can occur if public policies are based on the simple-minded assumption that everything, or almost everything, can be entrusted to the marketplace. In the United States, laissez-faire had been dead in practice for a long time; even eight years of Reaganism did not restore it to life. So Americans continue to be engaged, as they have been for generations, in attempts to find a more acceptable balance between market and nonmarket arrangements. I strongly doubt, however, whether Americans, or people in any other democratic country, will ever manage to arrive at a point where market and nonmarket forces are all at a stable equilibrium, politically speaking. The society, including the economy, is too dynamic to allow for permanence in public policies.

4. The experience of the democratic countries with the most advanced economies also tells us that no single pattern, or even a dominant one, has emerged; and what has emerged is a product of the special characteristics and the unique history of each country. Thus the Scandinavian countries together with Austria, Germany, and the Netherlands, among others, developed what are sometimes called systems of democratic corporatism. The expression *democratic corporatism* is used because economic policies of exceptional consequence were made, more or less beyond the reach of parliaments, by agreements among the major corporate entities, in particular, the trade unions and employers' associations, sometimes together with organizations representing consumers or farmers. Yet not only did the patterns of democratic corporatism differ greatly among these countries, but in others, such as Britain and the United States, corporatist structures were comparatively weak, in part because unions and employers' associations were much less inclusive, more fragmented, and more decentralized. The point is that we do not have a single model of relatively satisfactory "market economies" to consider for possible emulation; instead we have many models. Each country's pattern to some extent reflects the country's unique, or, at any rate, far from general, conditions and history. Attractive as some of us may find the Swedish model, for example, we must not assume that it can be transferred to other countries, where the necessary conditions may not exist now or in the foreseeable future.

5. **Actual practices in the advanced democratic countries are, then, far too diverse and complex to be captured by ideologies.** Many years ago, Charles E. Lindblom and I argued that it had become increasingly difficult for thoughtful persons to find meaningful alternatives posed in the traditional choices between socialism and capitalism, planning and the free market, regulation and laissez-faire. Economic organization, we asserted then, poses knotty problems that can be solved only by painstaking attention to technical details.[2] I believe that experience since then strongly confirms this judgment. This does not necessarily mean "the end of ideology." But it does mean that no sensible person should expect an ideology to provide solutions to concrete problems. Probably more often than not, an ideology is not very helpful even as a general guide. To take one example, questions about property and the most suitable forms of ownership admit of no simple answers. "Public versus private ownership and control of the means of production" is no more than a simplistic slogan. Not only do "public" and "private" mask an almost infinite variety of possibilities, but no reasonable person—or society—would, after carefully examining the concrete possibilities in specific situations, conclude that any single form of ownership and control would invariably be superior to all others. Likewise, to pose the issue as "planning versus the market" is, in

the light of the experiences of advanced democratic countries, simply silly. A good deal of central planning exists in these countries, particularly in the form of fiscal, budgetary, and monetary controls. Yugoslavia, in contrast, furnishes an example of a "socialist" country where the absence or weakness of these instruments for central influence over the economy has led to disastrous economic consequences.

6. It seems obvious, then, that the search for solutions to the problems generated by a predominantly privately owned market-oriented society has been and will continue to be a major element in the political agenda of every democratic country. As in the past, the search will take place amid political controversy. And it should. For even if solutions often depend on technical knowledge, rarely if ever is technical knowledge enough. Alternative solutions invariably engage important values as well — equity, equality of opportunity, liberty, security, progress, and community solidarity, among others.

7. Because intelligent choices of public policies require both technical understanding and sensitivity to the values involved, in modern democratic countries a form of specialized intellectual activity has evolved that tends to combine both aspects of policy. And a rather new type of intellectual has developed to engage in this activity: the policy specialist. Although the locations and functions of policy specialists vary among the democratic countries, in the United States they are now located in major institutions of all kinds, not only in the executive branches of government at every level—national, state, and local—but in the Congress and the state legislatures and municipal councils, and in political parties, business firms, trade unions, lobbying organizations, independent research centers, and universities. Their numbers, variety, and differences in perspectives and institutional loyalties tend to ensure that expertise is not monopolized by any one group, such as the White House or a congressional committee.

To keep technical knowledge from becoming the monopoly of any particular group, we need to create and maintain a considerable measure of pluralism among organizations engaged in the analysis of public policies; and we need a supply of well-trained specialists to staff them. For this task, neither ideological perspectives, such as a belief in the need for democracy and a market economy, nor technical knowledge bearing on the specific problem at hand, whether that of economists, engineers, scientists, or whatever, will by itself be sufficient.

It is no simple or easy task to manage a market-oriented economy in such a way as to maximize its advantages, which are great, and to minimize its disadvantages, which are also great. How best to do so is, and surely will continue to be, a subject of continuing debate and political struggle. But if we are to avoid the mistake of the classical liberals whose ideas were formed in reaction to the failures of mercantilism and the Poor Laws, we should not react to the failures of state ownership and central direction of the economy in countries governed by authoritarian Marxist-Leninist regimes by concluding that the best alternative is to turn everything over to unregulated markets. Not only would this be a misreading of the experience of the advanced democratic countries; for any country that chose to follow this path it would be a misfortune.

CHAPTER FOUR

FROM PRINCIPLES
TO PROBLEMS

I t would be ingenuous in the extreme to suppose that one can move directly to a program of action from principles as general as those I have set out, for intelligent action requires not only general principles but also knowledge of concrete circumstances. Principles provide an orientation, not a path; a compass, not a map. Agreement on principles facilitates dialogue but does not automatically produce agreement on conclusions.

Finding an optimum balance among the criteria of Personal Choice, Competence, and Economy can hardly be a perfectly harmonious process. Nor can it be a once-for-all leap into permanent utopia. Arrangements that seem optimal today will seem inferior later on, either because they have undergone change, though the outward shell of forms persists, or because perspectives have changed, as when costs now ignored or held tolerable are later seen to outweigh the advantages.

Any attempt to measure the institutions of a country—any country —against the criteria of Personal Choice, Competence, and Economy is bound to turn up some pretty grievous departures from an optimum, from *my* prescription, anyway, for an optimum. Lack of space and, it had better be said, lack of competence make it impossible for me to discuss anything like all the problems these criteria raise. I would, however, like to mention three problems that seem to me of great gravity.

If in discussing them I seem to have the United States specifically in mind, this is not only because it is the country I know best and in whose past, present, and future I find myself most deeply involved but also because this country has allowed great departures from reasonable principles of authority to occur with all too little public challenge.

In most countries that have reached the plateau of polyarchy that I mentioned earlier, the opportunity to make effective personal choices is highly unequal. I am not so sanguine as to believe that these opportunities can ever be made perfectly equal. Nonetheless a causal factor of substantial importance in the inequalities I have in mind are inequalities in resources; and even if it is true that inequalities in resources probably cannot be entirely eliminated, they can be substantially reduced.

Consider the axiomatics of the situation. In order to make an effective personal choice it is often necessary for you to influence other people to do or not to do something—for example, to let you take twenty-five dollars worth of groceries out of the store. To influence other people, ordinarily you need resources: twenty-five dollars, say, or a gun, to offer examples of the two most familiar political resources, money and violence. But there are many other resources—guile, for example, or access to legal authority.

To the extent that the resources needed to influence people are unequally distributed, the capacity to make personal choices effective is unequally distributed. For one obvious example, take the ballot. To be able to vote in a fairly conducted election is a political resource of considerable importance, which is why Marx and Engels came to urge workers to demand and use the suffrage. If you grant the suffrage to some people and not others, or give some persons more votes than others, then opportunities for making effective personal choices are, in this respect, unequal. This was a point on which white southerners had no doubts and why they used fraud and force to reverse Reconstruction and deprive black southerners of their newly gained suffrage. The market furnishes an even clearer example. The sensitivity of the market to its customers is both its virtue and its vice; the more sensitive the market is to customers, the more it must reflect differences in their capacity to spend.

To the extent that the capacity to make personal choices effective is unequally distributed, then freedom and opportunity are also unequal, and political equality is impaired.

All this is axiomatic. Yet these propositions, which surely are taken for granted by every thoughtful person, have to be juxtaposed with another so obvious that no one seriously contests it: in the United States as in many other countries a number of resources are distributed in extremely unequal fashion. From which it follows — again the conclusion is, so far as I know, unchallenged — that the opportunity to make effective personal choices, and hence the degree of individual freedom and opportunity, are markedly unequal.

So far I have been speaking of the general problem of effective choice. The problem is at its most acute in a democratic association, where political equality is prescribed as a norm. That differences in resources tend to subvert political equality, and great differences tend to subvert it completely, are propositions that have always been pretty much taken for granted. From Aristotle to Jefferson, it was axiomatic that you cannot maintain rule by the people except in a society where resources are rather equally distributed. Extreme inequalities, it was assumed, must beget oligarchy or despotism. Fearful of the poor, the rich will impose oligarchy, while the poor, fearful of the rich, will be mobilized by a popular despot. The experience of the third world adds new evidence to this ancient hypothesis by demonstrating yet again that wherever inequalities are extreme, democratic regimes are likely to be rare, precarious, and ephemeral.

Yet the process of democratization that occurred in Europe during the nineteenth century and into the twentieth reveals an alternative possibility of profound relevance. Extreme inequality in resources need not inevitably produce oligarchy or despotism; it may, as it did in a number of European countries, trigger a process of democratization in the course of which oligarchies are displaced by polyarchies and many of the old inequalities are radically reduced, if not by any means eliminated.

In order for those who are politically weak to push through a crucial if still uncompleted process of democratization, they have to learn how to pyramid their political resources very much in the way that, in the economic realm, an aggressive young man-on-the-make sometimes manages to transform his personal situation from poverty to riches. Although the democratizing process was far from uniform, to take what was perhaps the most typical case, in some countries workers and their leaders began with one potential resource, their solidarity in the job market. With this as a starter, they acquired organization. With organization they turned to politics and in due time gained the suffrage. As Engels emphasized strongly during the last decade of his life, provided workers were cohesive, once they had the suffrage their numbers would give them considerable leverage in elections. Elections enabled them to elect representatives; representatives gave them leverage on government policy. Changes in policies meant, among other things, greater equalization of resources and influence. Thus in some European countries the process of democratization, a kind of bootstrap operation, redistributed resources as it went along. In the United States, however, the process was to some extent reversed, as some inequalities actually increased. I want to come back to this point in a moment.

Although the process has not produced anything like full equality in political resources either in Europe or in the United States, the history of transforming oligarchy into polyarchy argues strongly that further democratization is achievable. The problem in the United States is to focus on strategic inequalities and to increase the speed of change.

In fact, the prospects for continuing the process of democratization have been markedly improved by a change in the pattern of inequalities that has been brought about by previous democratization and by industrialization. When Aristotle, Jefferson, and others insisted that extreme inequality must lead to oligarchy or despotism, they were thinking of preindustrial, primarily agrarian societies. It is characteristic of agrarian societies that the ownership of land is a preeminent resource: people who own the most land are also likely to find themselves on the top of the heap in most other ways. They are likely to have the greatest wealth and income, the highest status, the most education, better knowledge of the intricacies of politics and social organization, better facilities for keeping in touch with others in (or beyond) their own social class, and, naturally, the greatest power. Inequalities and advantages are, in a word, cumulative. (This is the unintended but nonetheless profound sociological truth in "Unto every one that hath shall be given, and he shall have abundance; but from him that hath not shall be taken away even that which he hath"—Matt. 25:29.)[1]

Initially, industrialization did not so much transform cumulative distribution of inequalities as intensify it; it was this stage of early industrial society with its harsh pattern of cumulative inequalities that Marx and Engels witnessed, interpreted, and condemned. Their descriptions were accurate enough; their forecasts were not, for among other things, they did not foresee the emergence in late industrial and postindustrial societies of an important modification in the pattern of inequalities.

To be sure, advantages and handicaps tend to be cumulative in all societies. But in advanced industrial or postindustrial societies, particularly if they are governed by polyarchies, this general tendency is somewhat softened by another. Extreme deprivation is attenuated by government policies and rising incomes, while the inequalities that remain tend to become somewhat less cumulative and more dispersed. By dispersed I mean that persons who are poorer in some resources such as wealth and status often (not always) have access to others such as the ballot, their sheer numbers, their solidarity, their special knowledge, and even some amount of collective economic weight to throw around. By drawing on the resources they do have, the less advantaged can often (not always) acquire leverage and bargaining power.

Because inequalities, though persistent and frequently extreme, are considerably more dispersed in advanced societies, less advantaged groups often start with a resource base that gives them a degree of potential influence far greater than European workers began with in the nineteenth century.

The greatest obstacle to democratization and reducing inequalities in the United States is not that bugbear with which the Left, old and new, was invariably so obsessed, an elite of wealthy men, or even that military-industrial complex so much referred to, but rather the military – industrial – financial – labor – farming – educational –professional – consumer – over-and-under-thirty – lower-middle-upper-class complex that, for want of a more appropriate name, might be called the American people. One of the more perplexing contradictions of Americans is that we have inherited an ethos of egalitarianism so salient that until recently (when its seamy side began to show) foreigners from Crèvecoeur and Tocqueville to Bryce and Brogan invariably remarked upon it. Side by side with this egalitarian ethos and tradition, however, there has been a tolerance for inequalities that in some cases are far worse than now exist in a number of other countries. In fact, precisely while the citizens of many European countries were slowly transforming a system of oligarchy based on a narrow suffrage into a more broadly based polyarchy that came to preside over a welfare state, in the United States a society of farmers, in which the proportions at the extremes of poverty and riches were comparatively small, was converted into a society of owners, employers, and employees in which the extremes were considerably larger. It is altogether likely, then, that from the beginning of the nineteenth century to the end, while inequalities were being reduced in Europe, the United States actually retrogressed in the general level of inequality. Americans preserved the older public creed of equality but lost some of the reality. As is our wont, we closed the gap with extravagant talk. Departures from the creed were glossed over and even celebrated by double-talk and double-think.

As everyone knows, the most inhuman of these departures was not a product of the industrial revolution but antedated it. Very early there was built into the American creed of equality a special clause exempting from its application residents of this country, some of whom had been around for a very long time, who had the wrong skin color and ancestral origins. All possibilities of further democratization, and even of maintaining this country at its existing level of polyarchy, depend upon the speed with which this deeply rooted and singularly inhuman inequality can be eradicated.

If racial discrimination is, alas, all too much an authentic part of the American tradition, this cannot be said for certain other forms of inequality that Americans have come to tolerate with astonishing equanimity. There can be no doubt that what democrats like Jefferson and Madison counted on to sustain democracy in America was a general and pervasive equality of condition, a condition they believed existed among a people then constituted mainly of farmers and prosperous working folk. It was this equality of condition (among whites) that so forcefully struck Tocqueville when he visited this country to witness and explain the phenomenon of democracy in America. But the triumph of business and industry and the creed of the businessmen during and after the Civil War carried with it a new tolerance for extreme inequalities of wealth, income, and property that Jefferson and Madison I am certain would have found intolerable. At the end of the century the populists fought a rearguard battle to keep the business creed from overpowering the old Jeffersonian ideal of an egalitarian society made up of property holders. They lost both politically and ideologically. The upshot is that the most opulent society the world has known includes a substantial minority of people living in relative poverty.

In addition to race, then, there are some other visible places to begin any effort to reduce inequalities — gross disparities in incomes, for one. Incomes both before and after taxes are distributed more unequally in the United States than in a number of other advanced countries, including Australia, Britain, and Sweden.[2] The American income tax, in fact, does very little to reduce inequalities in incomes.[3]

The case against our tolerance of inequities attributable to inherited wealth is even stronger. There can hardly be any injustice more contemptible than that perpetuated by a society where the freedom and opportunities available to human beings at birth depend not on differences in inherited abilities (for in the face of so much evidence to the contrary no one has ever shown that children of wealthy parents are genetically superior) nor on any special contribution the one has made (for each has yet contributed no more than to be born) nor on any wrongdoing in the other (for each starts life equally innocent of guilt and evil) but, rather, on the accident of birth. The case for inherited wealth is hardly strengthened by the argument that wealth may be a burden or that Andrew Carnegie may very well have been right that "the parent who leaves his son enormous wealth generally deadens the energies of the son, and tempts him to lead a less useful and less worthy life than he otherwise would."[4] Although a large inheritance is a handicap that I suppose most people are prepared to accept stoically, there is no reason public policy should encourage a gift that is unwise if it damages the character of the innocent recipient, unfair if it confers special advantages on one who has done nothing to merit them, and wasted if it does not.

Here again, Americans are curiously tolerant of the inequalities in opportunities, freedom, and influence that inherited wealth create. Although there seems to have been a decline in the concentration of wealth since 1929, when the top one-half of 1 percent of all persons in the United States owned one-third of the wealth, it was nonetheless true that in 1983 the richest 10 percent owned almost three-fourths of the wealth of the country.[5]

I have stressed inequalities in wealth and incomes because they reveal how far this country falls short not only of an ideal but of an actual condition of equality that was taken for granted by democrats like Jefferson and Madison in the early years of the Republic. But there is another important reason for particularly stressing incomes. When we attempt to compensate for gross inequalities in incomes by means other than providing income itself, the result is likely to be a patchwork of irritating regulations enforced by bureaucratic agencies. It is exactly this that has helped make a mess of welfare in the United States. At one extreme, the range of personal choice is vastly increased by opulence; at the other it is drastically restricted not only by the deprivations inflicted by low income but by the enormous network of bureaucratic regulations and restraints that have bedeviled the life of the welfare recipient. Instead of providing the poor with unrestricted income with which they could make their own personal choices effective, our system of welfare payments has treated them as wards of the state incompetent to make their own decisions. Yet the central and most obvious implication of this experience might easily be lost sight of: extreme inequalities in income such as now exist in the United States mean extreme inequalities in capacity to make personal choices effective, and hence extreme inequalities in individual freedom. Bureaucratic regulatory devices may compensate for loss of income; they cannot compensate for loss of personal choice, freedom, dignity, and self-respect.

One could easily find other sources of crucial inequalities in political resources. The extravagant costs of campaigning, for example, mean that we have reached a point where the person of average means, not to mention a poor person, cannot reasonably aspire to the presidency (unless the individual happens to have a generous Croesus as a close friend). Campaign costs are turning the Senate into what it was often held to be a half-century ago, a rich man's club. I suppose that an American born in the modern equivalent of the log cabin might yet make it to the White House, but before trying, the would-be president had better be able to afford a mansion.

This is not the place to describe all the respects in which Americans are unequal in their resources of influence and power and the concrete inequalities in freedom and opportunity they produce. The central point is that an optimal solution to the problem of authority in American society can never be found unless resources are distributed much more equally than at present. In other countries the problem may be less acute or more acute. But no country that aspires to be a democracy can safely ignore the powerful tendency for resources to be distributed unequally among its citizens.

SECOND PROBLEM:
THE CORPORATE LEVIATHAN

Public Authority, Private Rulers
You would be hard put to find a more obvious candidate for testing against the criteria of Personal Choice, Competence, and Economy than the large privately owned business enterprises in the

United States—and none whose government is, by these criteria, so lacking in legitimacy. Yet Americans have all but abandoned any serious challenge to the appropriation of public authority by private rulers that is the essence of the giant firm. A book on the American corporation by Richard Barber perfectly illustrates the point. Barber's study is sober, thorough, searching, illuminating, and the author by no means lacks sympathy for his subject. As any honest observer of the corporation must, Barber establishes that the large corporation is a center of "concentrated private economic power" that neither the market nor the state regulates more than weakly. Yet he does not show us how this power can be tamed.

> For the near future the public may not like the effects of concentrated private power, but there is little it seems able to do about it, given the existing political and economic climate. Power has gravitated to the American corporate giants. They exercise it with some restraint, but realize that their future lies in forming a partnership with a government which need not be greatly feared as a regulatory policeman.[6]

The problem is rendered even more difficult by the rapid expansion of the international corporation. Until recently the private firm, though long a favorite spook of the orthodox Left and the extreme Right, for the most part played a rather marginal (though not necessarily trivial) role in world affairs, but the flourishing international corporation is for all practical purposes a new, shadowy, unregulated polity with resources greater than those of most nation-states.[7]

In a society that sought to arrange authority according to the criteria set out in the first part of this book, these new principalities would be an anomaly. Although the power wielded by their rulers can be obfuscated by the dreams of opulence they create, it cannot, I think, be rationally justified. I do not see how the anomaly can persist indefinitely. Unfortunately, when a serious demand arises for changes in the government of the corporation, it will be found that the orthodox alternatives hardly satisfy reasonable criteria better than the existing arrangements.

The Fractured Spectrum

In a rational society guided in all its arrangements for authority by the criteria of Personal Choice, Competence, and Economy, how would people look upon economic enterprise? I believe they would see an economic enterprise as a kind of association of all those who are affected by its activities. How such an association might best govern its particular enterprise according to the criteria of Personal Choice, Competence, and Economy would be looked upon as a concrete, practical question to be decided after taking into account the particular circumstances of the enterprise. Depending on these circumstances, the government of an enterprise could take many different forms. Just as people in such a society would think it irrational to believe that one form of democracy is invariably preferable to the others, so they would think it foolish to decide a priori that one form for governing economic enterprise is preferable to others in all circumstances. To debate "capitalism" versus "socialism" would seem as quaint and archaic as to debate whether primary democracy should completely replace polyarchy. In such a society it would seem natural and normal to give serious consideration to the possibility that the steel industry should be turned over to a state-owned corporation and the post office to a quasi-private corporation. Such questions would be thought of as more technical than ideological, problems less of principle than of practical judgment.

Doubtless a few Americans think this way, but overwhelmingly they do not. As everyone knows, in this country the prevailing ideology prescribes "private" enterprise, that is, firms managed by officials who are legally, if not de facto, responsible to private shareholders. Outside certain functions traditionally reserved to agencies of the state, it is widely taken for granted that the only appropriate form for managing economic enterprise is the privately owned firm. Being more pragmatic in their practices than in their ideology, Americans sometimes resort to other forms, but ordinarily the technical arguments in favor of an alternative must be of enormous weight to overcome the purely ideological bias in favor of the private firm.

It is as if we were color-blind to half the spectrum. It is as if city planners considered all the alternative ways by which a superhighway might be routed through a city with least damage and greatest benefit, without ever giving thought to the possibility of routing it around the city or not building it at all. It is as if we knew only Rousseau, but not Madison and Jefferson, as if we thought the range of democratic possibilities included committee democracy, primary democracy, and referendum democracy, but not polyarchy or delegated authority.

Why are Americans half color-blind when they look at economic enterprise? An important reason is that our history has left us without a socialist tradition. To be sure, the first labor party in the world appeared in the United States in 1828, and we have had socialist parties as long as any other country. But like many a successor, that first labor party vanished completely in a few years, and the socialist parties never managed to acquire enough of a following to make them a major force in American life. At their peak in 1912 they won 6 percent of the total presidential vote; in the depths of the depression in 1932 the total vote for all socialist parties was less than 4 percent. Why the United States was uniquely able to pass through its industrial stage without generating a major socialist movement is an interesting and complex historical question. But I do not wish to search for an explanation here. Let us ignore the causes and consider the consequence.

The consequence is, I think, a serious limit to our capacity for clearheaded public consideration of how economic enterprises should be governed. Because we have no socialist tradition, our debates about economic institutions nearly always leave some major alternatives—chiefly "socialist" alternatives—unexplored.

Not that socialism provides the answers. Socialists often do not even seem to put the right questions. But a socialist tradition helps fill in some of the missing shades of the spectrum. If Americans were as pragmatic as they are supposed to be, and less ideological than they are in fact, they would not need a socialist tradition to offset their ideological narrowness. But in their present condition, with a patch over one eye and myopia in the other, Americans find it more difficult than they should to see the whole range of possibilities for an economic enterprise.

The Illusion of Private Enterprise

Philosophers point out that if everything in the universe instantaneously multiplied or diminished in size, we should have no way of knowing it. Something like this seems to have happened in this country. A nation of farmers with a sprinkling of merchants became a nation of employees, managers, and owners. The small family enterprise run by its owner became the large enterprise in which operation was separated from ownership. The ideology of the private enterprise of farmer and small merchant was transferred more or less intact to the big corporation. The sanctity of the private property owned by the farmer and small merchant became sanctified in the "private" property of the corporation. Because a nation of farmers had believed in the virtues of private enterprise, a nation of employees continued to accept the virtues of "private" enterprise.

The transfer of the old ideology to the new economy required a vast optical illusion, for nothing could be less appropriate than to consider the giant firm a *private* enterprise. Whatever may be the optimal way of governing the great corporation, surely it is a delusion to consider it a private enterprise. Consider General Motors. With gross sales in 1988 larger than Sweden's gross national product; with gross revenues in that year larger than those of the central government of the Netherlands; with employees and their families larger than the populations of a third of the countries in the world today; wholly dependent for its survival during every second of its operations on a vast network of laws, protection, services, inducements, constraints, and coercions provided by innumerable governments, federal, state, local, foreign, General Motors is de facto the public's business. It is hardly to be wondered at that the head of General Motors could have believed, and what is more uttered in public, that what is good for General Motors is good for the United States. In the circumstances, to think of General Motors as *private* instead of *public* is an absurdity.

It would be more realistic to think of all economic enterprise as a public service. Thought of in this perspective, a private economy is a contradiction in terms. Every economy is a public or social (not socialist) economy. To think about economic enterprise in this way does not automatically answer the question how an economic enterprise should be governed. But it does compel one to ask the question.

Conventional Nonsolutions
How *should* the large corporation be governed?

In any modern economy, whether you label it capitalist, socialist, mixed, or whatever, an enterprise is subject to three broad kinds of controls. There are the controls exercised by those who directly manage or run the firm. Let me call these *internal* controls. There are the controls exercised by other enterprises and economic entities, suppliers, consumers, rivals. These controls sometimes operate through the complex mechanisms of the market, sometimes through bargaining, collusion, collaboration, and so forth. For convenience, I shall call these *economic* controls. Finally, there are the controls exercised by various governments—state, local, provincial, national —*governmental* controls, if you like.

Now it is an arresting fact that the intellectual magicians who manipulated the grand theories about economic enterprises that dominated the public stage for over a century all had a clever way of making one or two of these controls mysteriously disappear. In a magic show, mystification is a good thing, but it is hardly to be commended in an economic program.

The neoclassical economists viewed internal controls, authority within the firm, rather as astronomers regard the gravitational force of the earth. To the astronomer, the earth's gravity is all concentrated at a theoretical point approximately at the center of the globe; from the astronomer's purely professional perspective, all the bustling life, struggle, force, and drama going on at the earth's surface are matters too trivial to be noticed. A revolution, a volcano, a hurricane, an earthquake may destroy his observatory, but *en principe* these things do not matter. In quite the same way, the neoclassical economists reduced the firm to an infinitesimal theoretical point in space where the particularities of Mr. Gradgrind or John D. Rockefeller had no more relevance than the living earth does to the astronomer. The complex government of the firm vanished and reappeared as the single rational entrepreneur pressed on by a lust for profit and an inhuman capacity for responding shrewdly to the impersonal forces of the market. As a classroom exercise this provided an opportunity for the virtuoso of the blackboard, but it told nothing about how General Motors should be governed or was governed. For that matter, the effects on lung cancer of the "rational" calculations of the cigarette manufacturers are a matter for which a display of fancy cost curves hardly constitutes a satisfactory answer.

Great advocates of the division of labor, the neoclassical economists assumed that the government of a firm was a matter for lawyers to handle. As it happens, lawyers have helped to work out an answer, one that seems to be taken for granted by most Americans. This, the orthodox "private property" view, says that the firm ought to be governed by the people who own it. The lawyer's answer may do for small businesses, the famous corner grocery run by mama and papa. But as an answer to the problem of the large corporation it is barely an improvement on the economists' nonanswer, for who owns the large corporation? The stockholders. And to argue that the large corporation should be governed by the stockholders is highly unpersuasive for two reasons.

In the first place, a moment's thought will show that it is an unreasonable denial of the Principle of Affected Interests. Why should people who own shares be given the privileges of citizenship in the government of the firm when citizenship is denied to other people who also make vital contributions to the firm? The people I have in mind are, of course, employees and customers, without whom the firm could not exist, and the general public, without whose support for (or acquiescence in) the myriad protections and services of the state the firm would instantly disappear. The Principle of Affected Interests gives these people a strong prima facie case for citizenship.

That the stockholder has a privileged status in the government of the firm is an anachronistic result of the fact that ownership, authority, and productive work in an enterprise were once united in the same persons. Historically, to own something meant to possess the right to use it as one saw fit under the general protection and regulation of the state. To an America of small farmers and small businesses, this conception naturally appeared to have great validity. What you owned, it seemed reasonable to suppose, was the product of your own labor. Elementary justice seemed to support your authority over it, your right to do what you pleased with it, subject only to certain legal limits laid down by the state. "In that original state of things, which precedes both the appropriation of land and the accumulation of stock, the whole produce of labor belongs to the laborer." This is not Marx speaking, but Adam Smith in *Wealth of Nations*.[8] The appropriation of land by private owners, and the need of laborers for capital that they could not themselves supply, created claims against "the whole produce of labor," for rent to landlords and for profit to capitalists. So far, Smith and Marx were in perfect accord. What Marx did, however, was nothing more nor less than to interpret rent and profit as illegal seizure of the "surplus value" created by labor; because they seized this surplus value, landlord and capitalist were not benefactors but exploiters of labor.

The socialist challenge touched off a lasting debate over the proposition that a person is entitled to own something used by another to furnish the owner a profit. Strictly speaking, the affirmative may not have won the debate. But its proponents won the battle of law and policy, and owners preserved the legal right to claim the profits of an enterprise, which was perhaps all most of them really cared about.

Paradoxically, however, not only Marx but socialists in general helped the defenders of the orthodox view to gain acceptance for one of the great myths of the nineteenth century. This was the myth that ownership, internal control, and legal rights to the profits of an enterprise all *had* to be united in the same persons. The myth obviously served the owners, but it also proved to the satisfaction of socialists that in order to control the firm, and thus acquire the authority to eliminate or otherwise affect profits, ownership has to be shifted to "the public," which in practice means the state.

Neither socialists nor antisocialists seriously challenged the mythology of ownership. Thus one question that had desperately needed to be asked was generally passed over: would it not be possible to split apart the various aspects of "ownership," so that internal control of the firm might be split off from those who claimed the profits? If so, why should citizenship in a firm be linked exclusively to the right to receive the profits of the firm?

By now, the first question has been answered by a resounding and incontrovertible yes. And that yes is the second flaw in the orthodox view. For orthodoxy is flatly belied by the reality of the modern corporation. Even if the owners of a large firm have the legal right to run it, everyone knows today that they do not and cannot run it. The question that was not asked during the great debate over socialism versus capitalism has now been answered: ownership has been split off de facto from internal control. Every literate person now rightly takes for granted what Berle and Means established decades ago in their famous study *The Modern Corporation and Private Property*: that increasingly in the large corporation ownership is separated from internal control. To be sure, stockholders do retain a nominal right to participate in governing the firm, but they do not and ordinarily cannot exercise that right. The role of the stockholders in the government of the large corporation is rather like that of the British monarch in investing the prime minister with office: the stockholders serve the purely symbolic function of conferring legitimacy and legality on a government that has managed to acquire power by other means. Unlike the British system since 1688, the American corporation occasionally suffers a palace revolution or coup d'état. As in old-fashioned military coups in Latin America, when one group of rulers is exchanged for another the structure of hierarchic authority under the managers remains unchanged.

Thus the traditional private property view of authority in the corporation denies the right of citizenship in corporate government to all the affected parties except the one group that does not, will not, and probably cannot exercise that right. If property ownership is necessarily attached to the right of internal control, then the modern corporation must be owned de facto not by the stockholders but by the managers. But if property ownership does *not* carry with it the right of internal control, then the stockholders have no special claim to citizenship, and very likely no reasonable claim at all.

If the orthodox private property answer is inadequate, unfortunately the orthodox socialist answer is little better. Over the period

of a century and a half since the term has come into use, socialism
has meant many things, and I do not want to cavil over definitions.
One prominent kind of old-fashioned socialism held that a solution
to many problems, including the government of the enterprise, was
to be found in "public ownership of the means of production." The
usual interpretation of this idea was to have the enterprise owned by
the state and managed by state officials. What should have been
perfectly obvious, but became so only after some industries were
nationalized in a number of European countries, is that this solution
left the hierarchical structure of authority intact—or strengthened
it. The U.S. postal system, after all, is hardly a model of democratic
government. Thus the traditional socialist answer ran directly counter
to another set of ideas that intersected with socialist thought, the
belief in "industrial democracy."

Why socialists were unable to see that "public ownership and
operation" might be very different from "industrial democracy" is a
fascinating and important chapter in social and intellectual history
for which there is no room here. A few aspects, however, are so
relevant to the question we are concerned with that they ought to be
emphasized. As we have seen, many socialists had an exaggerated
notion of the importance of "property" in the sense of "ownership."
The evils they saw in the business firm seemed to flow from the fact
that it was privately owned. Ergo: change enterprises from "private"
to "public" ownership, and presto! all will be well. But, they asked
themselves, how can the "public" own anything except through the
state? Hence, they reasoned, public ownership means state ownership. And since they took for granted that "ownership" means, among
other things, the right to manage the firm, the state would naturally
acquire the right to manage the firm. Having that right, it would use
it—in the interests, of course, of the public.

But just as we have learned that the private owners of a large
corporation do not govern it, even if they have nominal citizenship
rights, so we have learned that government ownership does not necessarily mean that the public, or even that part of the public most
affected by the operation of a firm, will have very much to do with
governing it. In the Soviet Union, for example, the general "public,"

as distinct from state officials, had no more to say about the government of enterprises than the general "public" in the United States
has to say about the government of General Motors; and workers
had even less say there than in this country.

That socialists who sympathized with industrial democracy ended
up by supporting bureaucratic centralization was also a result of
their fascination with the nation-state. Among those whom Marx
contemptuously labeled utopians, like Fourier and Owen, socialism
was envisaged as a decentralized system, for the socialist economy
was to consist of a multiplicity of small autonomous associations.
After Marx, the tendency was to lean heavily on the state, not perhaps the bourgeois state, possibly a workers' state, a state that might
wither away in some remote future, but in any case the state. In
countries like England and Sweden where socialist ideas were not so
deeply influenced by Marx, labor-socialist parties nonetheless
reflected the general confidence of their fellow citizens that the state
was a useful, trustworthy, and effective instrument of rule. Thus
socialists were caught up in the centralizing trends of the nineteenth
century. Just as liberal reformers turned to the nation-state as the
best instrument of reform and regulation, so the socialist leaders
placed their hopes, however much their rhetoric sometimes con-
cealed it, in the possibility of using the government of the nation-
state to run the economy. Like most reformist liberals, socialists came
to see in demands for decentralized institutions of government a
mask for privilege and reaction, or the bold, wild face of anarchism,
or, like the proposals of Guild Socialists in England, quaint ideas of
academic intellectuals. Their prejudice was far from absurd, but
whatever their intentions, the upshot was that socialism contributed
its own thrust toward bureaucratic centralization and away from
industrial democracy. In politics, as we all know, intentions and consequences are poorly correlated, and idealism has never been a protection against that.

Probably nothing strengthened the impetus of socialists toward
bureaucratic centralization more than their implacable rejection of
economic controls in general and the market in particular. Because
they could not envisage a vital coordinating role for economic con-

trols, they were trapped into dependency on the state. Being dependent on the state, they had to reject industrial democracy, for in the absence of economic controls, the only coordinating mechanism that remained was governmental control. But coordination by governmental control was obviously inconsistent with autonomy and self-government in the firm. What would industrial democracy do to the sacred central plan?

That the market might be usable under socialism; that if incomes were justly distributed, the market might enormously expand opportunities for the exercise of personal choice; that by decentralizing decisions to semiautonomous enterprises the market could provide a powerful force to counter bureaucratic centralization; that far from being the formless, anarchic, antisocial force portrayed by orthodox socialists, the market could be made into a highly sensitive instrument for coordinating myriads of activities too complex ever to be settled wisely by central planners — all this socialists did not understand. They were too perceptive to turn away from industrialization because it was a part of the bourgeois order. But in their ignorance they turned away from the market, believing it to be an inherent evil of capitalism that could have no place in a socialist order.

Thus the orthodox socialist answer was, and remains, as full of defects as the other, for it was bound to leave the hierarchical structure of the enterprise intact. What is more, workers confronted by their new bosses, now officials of the state, would henceforth be deprived of the legitimacy, and very likely the legality, of challenging their bosses in the old way by striking. Whether workers might be worse off or better off under bureaucratic socialism, one thing is clear. Socialism of this kind could never bring industrial democracy.

Self-management versus Interest Group Management

If both the private property and socialist solutions are unacceptable, are we stalemated? Understandably, in both the United States and the Soviet Union defenders of the status quo would like everyone to think so, for in that case the status quo — the pseudo-private corporation in the United States, the pseudo-public enterprise in the Soviet Union — would stand a much better chance of being preserved.

Probably the most radical alternative to the American and Soviet status quo was exemplified by the system of self-management that developed in Yugoslavia after its break with the Soviet Union in 1948. In fact, Yugoslavia's leaders introduced social self-management as a deliberate and systematic effort to shift from the orthodox, highly centralized, bureaucratic Soviet-style economy toward a socialism that would be more democratic, liberal, humane, and decentralized. Thus Yugoslavia became the only country in the world where a serious effort was made to translate the old dream of industrial democracy into reality—or into as much reality as dreams usually are.

Let me quickly add several large dark blotches to what might otherwise look like a rather rosy picture. I have already mentioned that in their headlong rush from the overcentralized economic systems that then prevailed elsewhere in communist countries, the communist leaders of Yugoslavia failed to provide for the kinds of central controls over fiscal, tax, and monetary policy that were, ironically, standard in the "free-market" countries of Western Europe. In their desire to construct a kind of market socialism, they not only rejected the Soviet model but largely ignored the experience of the most advanced capitalist countries where, as I pointed out in the last chapter, the limitations of an unregulated market economy were better understood. The results were, as I have said, disastrous.

Second, the leadership was not at all prepared to transform Yugoslavia into a Western-style democracy, a polyarchy. The leadership refused to allow an opposition party to exist; as the famous cases of Djilas and Mihailov soon revealed, merely to advocate an opposition party could land one in jail.

Third, massive differences among the six constituent republics and two autonomous provinces, often accompanied by deep historical antagonisms, made many Yugoslavs justifiably fearful that political democratization and liberalization would lead to the breakup of the country—a view that may have long delayed the advent of democracy.

Thus the Yugoslav experiment with self-management offers us little more, at best, than a suggestive hint of possibilities elsewhere. Nonetheless, some aspects of the attempt to establish a system of worker self-management in Yugoslavia suggest several questions relevant to our concerns here. At the heart of the system was the requirement that every firm be governed by councils elected by all the workers in the firm. The councils could and nearly always did choose managers who made day-to-day decisions and many longer-range decisions as well. The workers' councils seem to have produced an economy that by almost any standard was rather highly decentralized. And they generated a substantial amount of participation by workers in the government of the firms. To be sure, the workers' councils were by no means autonomous; here as elsewhere in Yugoslavia organized party opposition was not permitted, strikes were rare and of doubtful legality, and the special influence of the party was important. Nonetheless, it seems clear that the councils were much more than a façade behind which the party and state officials actually managed the enterprise.

What happens to "property rights" in such a system? Who *owns* the enterprise? In this kind of system the great myth of the nineteenth century stands exposed; ownership is dissolved into its various components. What is left? A kind of ghostly penumbra around the enterprise. The enterprise was described in the constitution as "social property." But it might be closer to the mark to say that *no one owned the enterprise*. It was not, certainly, owned by the state or by shareholders. It was not owned by the workers in the enterprise. The point is that "property" is a bundle of rights. Once the pieces in this bundle have been parceled out, nothing exactly corresponding to the conventional meaning of ownership or property remains.

How well would such a system satisfy the Criterion of Competence? To be specific, would the employees of large firms in the United States manage their enterprises competently? Would American enterprises be as efficiently run as at present? I think one ought to keep in mind that even a modest decline in physical productivity could be offset by some important gains, of which the most significant would be to transform employees from corporate subjects to citizens of the enterprise. How great a gain this would be depends on how much value we (and the employees) attach to democratic participation and control, how much we see these as good both intrinsically and in their consequences for self-development and human satisfaction, quite independently of other outputs. In the absence of strictly relevant experience, predictions about productivity are, of course, hazardous. As to the consequences for productivity of the various less radical schemes of employee participation and consultation that have been tried out in this country and elsewhere, the evidence is inconclusive.[9]

But surely the most relevant consideration is that in the United States management is increasingly professional and therefore available for hire. In fact, the emerging practice in the American corporation is for managers and even management teams to shift about among firms. As Barber writes:

> the old notion that a responsible official stays with his company, rising through the ranks and wearing the indelible badge of Ford or IBM or duPont, is quaint and out of tune with a world of skilled scientific business management. It is not that the new executive is any less interested in or dedicated to the success of the company that employs him; rather it is that he sees himself as a specialist whose skills and growth are in no way necessarily associated with any particular enterprise.[10]

I do not see why a board of directors elected by the employees could not select as competent managers as a board of directors selected by banks, insurance companies, or the managers themselves. The board of a self-governing firm might hire a management team on a term contract in the same way that a board of directors of a mutual fund often does now. Surely if the profit motive is all that it has been touted to be, who has more at stake in improving the earnings of an enterprise than employees would have if the management were responsible to them rather than to stockholders?

Moreover, the development of professional managers starkly spotlights the old question *Quis custodiet ipsos custodes?* As Barber points out:

> With corporate managers holding the reins of widely diversified, global firms, but conceiving of themselves essentially as pro-

fessionals, what are the rules — the standards — with which these men are to be governed in their use of the immense power they possess? As well, how are those *within* the corporation — especially its multitudinous family of technocrats and middle-level executives — to be protected from encroachment on their legitimate interests?[11]

Although Barber poses the question, he offers no answer. Yet self-management is one solution too obvious to be ignored — except in a country blinded by an unthinking adherence to the absolute conception of a "private" firm "owned" by stockholders.

It is not, I think, the Criterion of Competence but rather the Criterion of Personal Choice that raises problems for self-management. These problems arise because of the possibility that many employees may not wish to participate in the government of the firm, and many people not employed in the enterprise could claim a right to participate under the Principle of Affected Interests.

Consider the people who work in the enterprise. Although many employees, particularly technicians and lower executives, would probably welcome self-management, it is very much open to doubt, unfortunately, whether blue-collar workers want to allocate any of their attention, time, and energy to governing the enterprises in which they work. Although sentimentalists on the Left — if any remain — may find the idea too repugnant to stomach, quite possibly in the United States workers and trade unions are the greatest barriers at present to any profound reconstruction of economic enterprise. Several aspects of their outlook militate against basic changes. Along with the officialdom of the trade union movement, workers are deeply ingrained with the old private property view of economic enterprise. What is perhaps more important, affluent American workers, like affluent workers in many advanced countries and the middle class everywhere, tend to be consumption-oriented, acquisitive, privatistic, and family-centered. This orientation has little place for a passionate aspiration toward effective citizenship in the enterprise (or perhaps even in the state!). The job is viewed as an activity not intrinsically gratifying or worthwhile but rather an instrument for gaining money that workers and their families can spend on articles of consumption. In this respect, modern workers have become what classical economists said they were: economic beings compelled to perform intrinsically unrewarding, unpleasant, and even hateful labor in order to gain money to live on. So far as its intrinsic rewards are concerned, work is simply so much time lost out of one's life. The workplace, then, is not your small society; it is simply a place where you put in time and labor in order to earn money. The union is a necessary instrument, but it is also a crashing bore. Solidarity is a matter of sticking together during bargaining and strikes in order to get better wages, but it is not animated by any desire to change the structure of power within the firm.

The upshot for many workers is that a chance to participate in the government of the enterprise (even during working hours) might very well hold slight attraction. After all, in polyarchies and primary democracies a great many citizens are indifferent toward their opportunities to participate; so long as the enterprise pays good wages, its affairs seem even less interesting than affairs of state. In addition to reflecting these attitudes of their constituents, trade union leaders could easily interpret self-management as a threat to their influence: the consequences for incumbent leaders would at best be uncertain, and like leaders generally, most trade union leaders prefer to avoid risks.

Yet these bleak prospects are by no means the whole story. The impetus toward self-management may not come from the strata the conventional Left for so long courted. It may come instead from the white-collar employees, technicians, and the executives themselves. What is more, there is a good deal of evidence to show that although participation does not guarantee increased output in the conventional sense, it does generally increase workers' satisfaction with and interest in their work situation. If a significant number of employees, whether white-collar or blue-collar, were to discover that participation in the affairs of the enterprise — or that part of the enterprise most directly important to them — contributed to their own sense of competence and helped them to control an important part of their daily lives, then lassitude and indifference toward participation might change into interest and concern. Of course, we should not entertain excessive expectations. Nor should we reject self-management because it may not measure up to the highest ideals of participation—ideals that are, after all, not met in any democratic association.

The most severe problem raised by the Criterion of Personal Choice is, I believe, the existence of Affected Interests other than the employees of the enterprise: not only consumers but others who may be affected by decisions about location, employment, discrimination, innovation, safety, pollution, and so on. How can these Affected Interests be sure that their claims will be fairly weighed in the decisions of the firm? By focusing attention on the state as the best agent of all the Affected Interests, this question often drives the advocate of change straight onto the horns of the old dilemma: either bureaucratic socialism or else the private property solution. It is precisely because self-management enables us to escape this dilemma that it is so hopeful an alternative. Have we then escaped the dilemma only to find it lying in wait farther down the road?

I shall not pause to argue with any reader, if there be one, who is so unworldly as to suppose that once "the workers" control an enterprise they will spontaneously act "in the interests of all." Let me simply remind this hypothetical and I hope nonexistent reader that if self-management were introduced today, tomorrow's citizens in the enterprise would be yesterday's employees. Is their moral redemption and purification so near at hand? If not, must self-management wait until workers are more virtuous than human beings have ever been heretofore? For my part it seems wiser to design a government on the assumption that people will not always be virtuous and at times surely will be tempted to do evil, yet where they will not lack for the incentive and the opportunities to act according to their highest potential.

We can now see how the distinction I made earlier between internal controls, economic controls, and government controls suggests roughly three ways—not mutually exclusive—for satisfying the Principle of Affected Interests.

To begin with, in addition to workers other Affected Interests may be given the right to participate in internal controls, to have a direct say in management—for example, through representatives on the board of directors of the enterprise. Let me call this solution *interest group management.*

Now whatever may be the case in other countries, candor compels me to admit that interest group management seems much more in the American grain than self-management. It fits the American ethos and political culture, I think, to suppose that conflicting interests can and should be made to negotiate: therefore let all the parties at interest sit on the board of directors. It would be a very American thing to do. Interest group management is, then, a much more likely development in the United States than self-management. I can readily see how we may arrive incrementally at interest group management of giant firms. Since this innovation would probably be enough to deflate weak pressures for further change, the idea of self-management would be moribund.

Yet even if interest group management is more likely in the United States, it is much less desirable, in my view, than self-management. For one thing, interest group management does very little to democratize the internal environment of an enterprise. Instead, it would convert the firm into a system of rather remote delegated authority, for there is no democratic unit within which consumer representatives, for example, could be elected and held accountable. The delegates of the Affected Interests doubtless would all have to be appointed in one way or another by the federal government, by organized interest groups, by professional associations. There would be the ticklish problem of what interests were to be represented and in what proportions—a problem the Guild Socialists struggled with, but never, I think, solved very satisfactorily. Since the consequences of different decisions affect different interests, have different weights, and cannot always be anticipated, what particular interests are to be on the board of management, and how are they to be chosen? Are the employees to elect a majority or only a minority? If their representatives are a majority, the representatives of other Affected Interests will hardly be more than an advisory council. If a minority, I fear that most people who work for large enterprises would be pretty much where they are now, remote from the responsibility for decisions.

Doubtless interest group management would be an improvement over the present arrangements, and it may be what Americans will be content with, if the corporation is to be reformed at all. Yet it is a long way from the sort of structural change that would help reduce the powerlessness of the ordinary American employee.

Moreover, interest group management would not eliminate the need for economic and governmental controls. Is it not through these, rather than by participating in internal controls, that the Affected Interests could best be represented and protected in a system of self-management?

I cannot stress too strongly the importance of external controls, both governmental and economic. I do not see how economic enterprises can be operated satisfactorily in a modern economy, capitalist, mixed, socialist or whatever, without some strategic external controls over the firm. It is worth keeping in mind, too, that the less effective the external economic controls are—the influence of customers and suppliers on costs and prices, suppliers of capital and credit on interest rates and terms of borrowing, competing firms and products on the growth and prosperity of the enterprise—the greater must be the governmental controls. Just as the extreme limit of economic controls is the fully competitive economy (whether capitalist or socialist), so the extreme limit of governmental controls is bureaucratic socialism. The optimum combination of internal, governmental, and economic controls will not be easy to find.

Yet it seems obvious that if we place much value on democracy at the workplace, the present arrangement is ludicrously far from optimal. As for alternatives, self-management seems to me closer to the optimal than bureaucratic socialism or interest group management.

THIRD PROBLEM:
THE DEMOCRATIC LEVIATHAN

Polyarchy in Perspective

When one thinks about democracy as an ideal, I suspect that what most often comes to mind is something like committee, primary, or referendum democracy. But when one thinks about democracy as an accomplishment, I imagine that one is more likely to envision the institutions of polyarchy.

Because polyarchy is light years distant from achieving the fullest possibilities of primary democracy, I must say a few words to put this gap in perspective. Although polyarchy shows up badly compared with unrealized ideal forms, it looks very much better when it is compared with other political systems that have actually existed up to the present. In particular, when it is placed alongside rival political forms that have been tried out in this century—waves of the future that swept the people overboard—polyarchy looks to be not only incomparably closer to genuine rule by the people but much more humane, decent, tolerant, benign, and responsive in dealing with citizens.

The antique trademark of the state is coercion. And polyarchies have most definitely not eliminated coercion. In dealing with persons who are de jure or de facto excluded from citizenship—foreigners, colonials, people in enemy countries, and, in the United States for a full century after the Civil War, southern blacks—polyarchies have yet to show that they are on the whole superior to the average run of states in the past. Yet polyarchies rarely adopt highly coercive measures (or if they do, rarely enforce them for long) against any group of citizens with recourse to the ballot and other processes of polyarchy. Taken all in all, in comparison with the alternatives cast up by history rather than by imagination, polyarchy must be appraised, I believe, as a superior instrument for achieving a decent government among a very large body of citizens.

That level of achievement seems to look higher to those who have experienced other regimes than to those who have not. In north-western Europe and the United States, the plateau of polyarchy was gained just long enough ago that the sense of triumphantly reaching new heights has turned into a feeling that we have been stuck too long on a tiresome plain. In a world distinguished by an incredible and unassimilable rate of novelty, polyarchy is inescapably old-fashioned. Those who witnessed vicariously or actually the destructive despotisms of Stalin and Hitler may recognize that if polyarchy is light years away from primary democracy it is also light years away from a truly despotic regime. But the perception of the first gap becomes sharpened and the second blurred for more recent generations to whom the inhumanities of Nazi and Stalinist rule seem as remote and irrelevant as the barbarities of Genghis Khan.

The Irreparable Flaw

Polyarchy suffers not only from having become familiar, routine, and old-fashioned in a world that feasts on novelty. It also has an irreparable flaw—the remoteness of the government (I have in mind chiefly the national government) from the citizen. For ordinary citizens participate little or not at all in many decisions that have crucial import for their lives.

What I want to emphasize are not the ordinary, and for the most part reducible, obstacles to effective participation. Everyone knows, or should know, that opportunities to participate are unequally distributed in the United States. In the extreme case, until the late 1960s in many parts of the Deep South a black person who tried to vote would have risked serious injury or even death; the audacity to run for office was an open invitation to the lynch mob. Even in countries where the familiar opportunities to participate are technically accessible and better protected than they have been in this country—in Sweden, for example—we know that some people do not seize the opportunities available to them, few people take advantage of all their opportunities, and the few who do gain much greater influence over decisions than the rest who do not. For several decades social scientists have been doing an enormous amount of research on political participation; as a result the most important causes for nonparticipation can now be pretty well specified. Many of these, and certainly the most unjust ones—registration and voting laws and practices that make participation unnecessarily difficult, discriminatory laws and practices, severe lack of education, inadequate organization and mobilization, apathy produced by poverty or a group history of subjection and defeat—can be eliminated or at the very least greatly reduced. Greater equality in political resources, which I emphasized at the beginning of this chapter, would reduce gross differences in opportunities for participating in decisions.

Of course, even in a highly egalitarian society one could still choose whether or not, and how much, to participate. As a result there would still be individual differences—more, I would guess, than many ardent political types believe possible. Yet in comparison with the present, these differences would result more from the exercise of personal choice over an array of opportunities and less from objective differences in the opportunities available.

What I have in mind is a rather different obstacle: it is one we have already encountered a number of times in these essays, though in different forms. It served as a backdrop for the play of the argument in chapter 2. At the risk of seeming to repeat myself, and to overstress an elementary axiom (I take the risk because the matter is so important), I want to lay heavy emphasis on a disagreeable fact about polyarchy, one of those disagreeable facts that will be readily admitted, no doubt, and yet, I fear, at once brushed aside: *severe upper limits are set on effective participation in "democratic" decisions by the sheer number of persons involved.* To put the same point in a different way, whenever large numbers of persons are affected by decisions, there are bound to be differences in opportunities to participate in those decisions, no matter how ready everyone is to democratize the procedures.

You were invited in chapter 2 to perform a little arithmetical exercise in order to see for yourself the drastic limits of primary democracy. Now I ask you to perform a similar exercise to see how drastic are the limits of participation in a large polyarchy. They are, after all, essentially the identical limits.

Choose a polyarchy of modest size, so as not to bias the presentation—Sweden, say, or if you want a city (only a little smaller in population), New York. Imagine that the citizens of Sweden or New

York amended their constitution in order to guarantee every citizen the right to participate in governmental decisions at any and every stage, through final enactment. Consider now the situation of the chief executive. Suppose that in order to fulfill his obligations under the new amendment the prime minister (or mayor, as the case may be) decides to set aside ten minutes for any citizen, or any group of citizens, wishing to see him about some matter. He details the task of working out a schedule to an assistant. Moments later, we may imagine, the assistant returns. (The arithmetic is simple, as you will see.) If the prime minister (or mayor) were to meet one person at a time, allow ten minutes for each meeting, and set aside one hour a day for meetings of this type every day of the year, in a year he could meet with about three-hundredths of 1 percent of the total population. Of course, by devoting ten hours every day of the year, he could meet with three-tenths of 1 percent. If instead of meeting only one person at a time he were to meet with groups of one hundred for ten minutes (participation, you notice, becomes pretty symbolic at this point), he could meet with 3 percent of the population in a year if he set aside one hour and met six groups every day, and 30 percent if he set aside ten hours and met sixty groups every day.

These are the limits, mind you, in a smaller country or a giant city. What would be an absurdity in a small country would be grotesque in a giant one. But no matter whether the amendment were adopted in a small country or a large one, with the best will in the world its consequences would remain purely symbolic. As an occasion for political comedy and an incentive for schoolchildren, journalists, and politicians to do their lessons in arithmetic it might do no great harm. It would be a disaster for a country that tried to take it seriously.

In discussing the Criterion of Economy, I showed that your judgment about optimal arrangements for authority should take into account the costs of time. You can now see how the costs of some arrangements that might be proposed, like our hypothetical constitutional amendment, could exceed all possible resources. In cases like this the limits set by time are absolute. It is not a matter of relative costs, of giving up one thing in order to gain something else, so that you can still have what you want if only you are willing to sacrifice enough other things. Some solutions are actually prohibited because the requirements of time exceed the time available in any circumstances. Just as there is quite literally no conceivable way by which every citizen of New York can be guaranteed an opportunity to speak at a meeting where every other citizen also speaks, so there is literally no way by which every citizen of New York or Sweden (let alone the United States) can be guaranteed the right to participate in decisions at every stage of the process.

No doubt many readers will take this conclusion for granted. There are people, however, who find it a brutal restraint on the democratic potential of polyarchy. For those to whom "democracy" means either primary democracy or cheap and shoddy substitutes, one escape is by way of magic. Magical solutions fall into two types: completely replace polyarchy in the large unit by primary democracy or completely replace units too large for primary democracy by units small enough for primary democracy. I hope that by now I do not need to explain why these solutions are illusory.

The magician who puts polyarchy into a hat and pulls out primary democracy may confound the very innocent and the true believer; everyone else sees that what looks like a town meeting of a hundred million people is pure razzle-dazzle. As for making all large political systems vanish into thin air, when the silk scarf is pulled away there in full sight are matters that cannot be handled by completely autonomous communes, neighborhoods, or villages: matters of trade, tariffs, unemployment, health, pollution, nuclear energy, discrimination, civil liberties, freedom of movement, not to say the whole tragic tangle of historically given problems like the threat of war and aggression, the presence of great military establishments around the world, the danger of annihilation. These problems inexorably impel us to larger and more inclusive units of government, not to small and totally autonomous units. In a world with so many interdependencies, the hope for democracy cannot rest on total autonomy but, as I argued earlier, on democratic systems constructed like Chinese boxes, the smaller nested in the larger.

So let us put away our infantile fantasies, the yearning to return to an infancy of the species that never was, where humanity existed in small and totally autonomous units like tribes or villages and practiced primary democracy and knew peace and harmony. It may be that if most inhabitants and the technological know-how already existing on humanity's fragile and crowded spaceship are consumed in a thermonuclear Judgment Day, the survivors might be able to exist, for a time, in tiny, fully sovereign, widely separated units. Only a madman would think that a solution. No, because the species *is* interdependent, giant political systems are a necessity. For my part, I cannot quite see how rule by the people could be approximated in large systems except by something very much like polyarchy.

An Ugly Dilemma
Still, even if polyarchy is desirable as an approximation to rule by the people where citizens number in the millions, the challenge is to make it a better approximation. At the end of chapter 2, I offered several pragmatic principles. Two of these will help as guides while we search for solutions to the problems of the democratic Leviathan.

1. If a matter is best dealt with by a democratic association, seek always to have it dealt with by the smallest associations that can handle it satisfactorily.
2. In considering whether a larger association might not be more satisfactory, always consider the extra costs of the larger, including the possibility that the sense of individual powerlessness will increase.

I have been aware all along, and no doubt the reader has too, that an ugly dilemma lurking in chapter 2 might rob these pragmatic principles of significance. The dilemma is this: because human beings are in various ways interdependent, to apply the Principle of Affected Interests requires, for some purposes, associations with memberships in the millions, hundreds of millions, perhaps even billions. Yet as we have just seen, the larger an association the more that sheer numbers prevent everyone from participating equally in decisions. The smaller an association, the more fully it can adhere to the principle of political equality. Yet the smaller an association, the fewer the problems it can cope with satisfactorily because of actions taken by people over whom it has no authority. At one extreme, then, an association large enough to include all the Affected Interests may be so huge that not even a faint approximation to equal participation is possible; at the other extreme an association may be so small that, as I said of the microstate in chapter 2, the people can rule but they have very little to rule over.

Two questions:

First, can we preserve or create units smaller than giants like the nation-state or megalopolis that have, or anyway could have, enough authority so that participating in their decisions would be truly important? I need hardly point out that even a satisfactory level of participation is impossible to achieve unless citizens have substantially equal resources, and in what follows I am going to have to assume that we have gone a good deal further than we have in solving this, our first problem.

The corporation seems to me just such a unit. But I want to explore the question whether there may not also be relatively small and yet vital territorial units in which a satisfactory level of participation is possible.

Second, let me now take for granted that whenever large numbers of people must be included in a democratic association, the institutions of polyarchy seem to provide the closest approximation we know to rule by the people. Still, are there not ways of making polyarchy a closer, a better approximation? Need I mention again the absolutely critical importance of a greater equalization of political resources? Nothing we can do would democratize polyarchy more. In addition, however, there is an institutional innovation that might help to democratize the Leviathan. Let me describe it briefly.

Participation by Lot

Selecting representatives by election has completely displaced selection by lot in modern democracies, so much so that a proposal to introduce selection by lot will almost certainly strike most readers as bizarre, anachronistic and—well, antidemocratic.

Nonetheless, I propose that we seriously consider restoring that ancient democratic device and use it for selecting advisory councils to every elected official of the giant polyarchy—mayors of large cities, state governors, members of the U.S. House and Senate, and even the president.

Let us imagine that the membership of each advisory council were to consist of several hundred constituents picked by the same procedures used to ensure randomness in modern sample surveys; that the citizen selected would be required to serve, as is supposed to be the case now with jury duty, though honored in the breach; that suitable provisions would ensure against hardships arising from the obligation to serve—for example, not only would the citizen selected have all relevant expenses taken care of, but the poor or unemployed person might receive a stipend, and an employed person would continue to receive his or her regular pay; that one would serve for a year and be ineligible for a second term; that a council might meet at intervals for a total of several weeks in the course of a year; that it would have its own presiding officer (and a professional parliamentarian); and that it would invite the elected official to meet with it to answer questions and hear the debate and discussion.

Anyone who has grown accustomed to thinking of the citizen in a polyarchy as more subject than citizen will no doubt be surprised by my proposal. Yet aside from the crime of lèse-majesté I do not see any problems that could not be met satisfactorily by the exercise of reasonable foresight before establishing the councils and by profiting from their experiences afterward.

If a conventional critic will say that the proposal goes too far, a less conventional critic will object that it does not go far enough. Why, one might ask, should the councils be only advisory? Why not go the whole way and let them have powers of decision? To put the question in a different way: why not choose our official representatives by lot rather than by election?

I would not want this objection swept aside, yet I think that the criteria of Competence, Economy, and Personal Choice argue against it. One hundred more or less average citizens snatched out of their daily lives by random selection would find the work of the U.S. Senate, for example, formidably complex. Incompetent as political lore describes our officials, it is romantic to suppose that a group of average citizens abruptly confronted by the need to make national decisions on appropriations, expenditures, revenues, foreign affairs, foreign trade, nuclear energy, and the hundreds of other matters the Congress deals with, could quickly acquire the organizational know-how and the substantive knowledge to arrive at equally competent decisions, or even to get round to making any decisions at all. One of the most depressing yet well-substantiated results of innumerable scientific surveys is to document how very thin and fragmented in content are the political views of the average citizen or, for that matter, the average voter. To account for the difference between the ordinary citizen's poverty of substantive knowledge in the domains of politics, government, and domestic and international affairs and the comparative richness of content in the views of the average elected official, we need not resort to innate differences in abilities or capacities but acknowledge the very considerable amount of highly motivated learning that generally precedes and follows tenure in public office. If elected officials were all replaced by citizens chosen by lot for short terms, I fear the contest between expert bureaucracies and legislative bodies would be even more unequal than at present. Far from increasing citizen control, as a simplistic advocate of democratization might contend, it would very likely increase the influence of skilled bureaucrats by a wide margin.

I can fairly hear some reader shouting that all I have been asserting about the average citizen does not apply to him or her! Dear reader, I agree. Should you object further that if persons like yourself were chosen for office, governing would be carried on with infinitely greater wisdom and justice than now, I would be disinclined to argue. But you have to recognize that the average person is not going to read this book, and your having reached this point in the argument proves to me that you are not very close to the average American in your degree of interest in politics, your capacity for handling abstractions, the amount of your substantive knowledge, and, probably, your familiarity with the ordinary rules of procedure in parliamentary bodies.

All right, then, you may say, why not select our representatives by lot and allow them long enough terms to acquire a more adequate understanding of public policy, like officials now elected for terms of two, four, and six years and reelected for many more? Unfortunately, this solution would create more problems than it would solve. For one thing, though the obligation to serve might perhaps be made obligatory if service were confined to a few weeks out of one year, it is quite inconceivable that service could be obligatory for the full-time, long-term duty now characteristic of members of Congress, mayors of large cities, and governors. If service were optional, the system no longer being random would lose much of its merit.

The Criterion of Economy also begins to intrude. For reasons I have already emphasized ad nauseam, and that create the very problem we are trying to solve, the number of persons who could participate effectively in an effective legislature can hardly be more than five or six hundred at most. Time's incorruptible balance means that the longer the terms of our randomly selected members, the fewer the number of citizens who could participate. You pays your money and you takes your choice.

Finally, the Criterion of Personal Choice argues against choosing all or most policy-making officials by lot in a polyarchy. In Athens, after all, the officials chosen by lot were subject to the Assembly. In the absence of elections, to whom would a legislature chosen by lot be subject? Since—as anyone familiar with the laws of probability knows—the chances are by no means negligible that a sample of five hundred might deviate by a considerable margin from the mean of the whole population, occasionally we might find ourselves with a highly unrepresentative legislature subject to no authority except the next lottery. I cannot think of a better way to discredit the idea and democracy itself.

We have now worked our way round to a conclusion that may be getting tiresome by its constant intrusion into these essays. Polyarchy *can* be further democratized, doubtless by still more means than those I have set out here or managed to think up. Nonetheless, there is not any magic by which polyarchy in a large country can be transformed into a reasonable approximation to primary democracy.

Noncitizens in Megalopolis

It must be pretty clear by now that if we want to reduce time's implacable constraints in order to increase opportunities for participation, we shall have to find ways by which citizens can participate more fully in smaller units, units smaller than nation-state or megalopolis. These smaller units must be, I think, neighborhoods and cities of human proportions. This means both preserving and creating. To move in this direction is to transform into terms appropriate to modern life a much older perspective on the human dimensions of an urban polity, a perspective that the explosive and fascinating eruption of megalopolis during the past century has all but buried from view.

As a place where any significant fraction of a country's population is expected to live, as a normal habitat for human life, the giant city, the urban concentration larger than a half million, let us say, is a very late arrival in human history. Before the mid-nineteenth century the overwhelming number of people in every country, including countries thought to be "modern," lived in towns and villages. The chances are really quite overwhelming that not one of your great-grandparents was born in a large city. Even today, in practically every country, big-city dwellers constitute a minority.

Because the very recency of the giant city has made it a symbol of modernization and modernity, particularly for developing countries, visions of a society with few if any giant cities are typically brushed off as nostalgic evocations of an irrecoverable past. Yet the "modernity" of the giant city derives from the age of industrialization, not from the more recent age of late or postindustrialization. In postindustrial society, the giant city becomes an obsolescent, unnecessary, and crippling habitat that persists less because of need than from inertia, sunk costs, a failure of imagination, and a lack of audacity.

So much is the giant city an elephantine perversion of the city that we have no suitable name for it. As if to mock us, the Latin roots of the word *city* remind us of what is most lacking in the giant city: citizenship; and origins of the term *metropolis* convey a meaning precisely opposed to present usage. Literally, *metropolis* means "mother city" (from the Greek *mētēr*, a mother, and *polis*, a city). Unlike us, the ancient Greeks assumed that no decent city should be permitted to grow indefinitely. A large city would outstrip its own resources, become unwieldy and ill proportioned, inconvenient, an unfit place for living, unsuitable for primary democracy, a habitat that must inevitably reduce citizens, who might hope to know their city and one another well, into anonymous inhabitants each dominated by private concerns and lacking common goals or interests — no true city, then, no polis, but a mere heaping up of people and buildings. To avoid this catastrophe was both desirable and possible. The polis invited its citizens, not least its youth, to join in establishing a new polis. So the original city gave birth to the new, and the original thus became the mother city, a metropolis. Thus cities of human proportion could be built and preserved.

Since we have no proper word for the giant city, shall we settle for the appropriately ugly term *megalopolis* (*megalo*, from the Greek *megas*, meaning large)?

I do not want to deny anyone who wants to live in megalopolis the opportunity to do so (provided, of course, that there are enough others who want the same thing to make megalopolis possible). But by the same token, those who prefer a different habitat ought to have that option. We know which option most Americans would take. And I do not think it a sign of backwardness or simple-minded nostalgia that when they are offered a choice most Americans express a preference for living in a unit smaller than megalopolis. The fact is that only a small minority of Americans say they prefer to live in a large city — and what they have in mind may be something closer to a half million than anything larger. The rest express a preference for suburb, small town, or country. Even the residents of the large city do not, in the main, live there from preference.[12]

Why should anyone be compelled by circumstances to live in megalopolis? As a habitat for the ordinary person, a city with a population less than a half million, and quite likely less than 100,000, appears to be capable of providing virtually all the advantages of megalopolis, with fewer disadvantages.[13] Possibly a case can be made for megalopolis as a transitional form between early and late or postindustrialization. Even on that score, the swollen, slum-infested cities of Latin America and Asia ought to give one pause. However that may be, in late or postindustrial society megalopolis is an economic, cultural, and political anachronism.

A cost-benefit analysis that conscientiously tried to weigh all the costs would probably not show it to be economically advantageous.[14] As for its cultural superiority, the idea that vast numbers of urban residents are needed to provide a center of creativity, innovation, and cultural amenities is unsupported by historical evidence. We ought never forget how very small the great cities of the Western world were when creativity flourished most. The ancient Greeks had only three cities with more than 20,000 male citizens (equivalent to a total population of perhaps 100,000). Two of these were in Sicily. Athens, the largest of all Greek cities and the only mainland city over 20,000, may have had as many as 40,000 citizens in Pericles' time and a total population not more than several hundred thousand at most. (The exact figure is unknown.) Throughout the Renaissance all the cities of Europe were comparatively small. Until 1600 there were only two cities (Naples and Paris) with populations over 200,000. Rome, Florence, and Venice each had less than 100,000 inhabitants. During the age of Elizabethan England, London had a population under 200,000. By the end of the sixteenth century, the inhabitants of Paris numbered a little over 200,000.

You may object that megalopolis is indispensable as a center of concentrated skills necessary for corporate headquarters or for certain uniquely cosmopolitan forms of entertainment and cultural activities. But since neither corporate executives nor cosmopolites are compelled to live in the city, and generally manage to escape it when it pleases them, to argue that the great mass of people must live in the undesirable and unwanted environment of megalopolis to provide satisfactions for the few seems to me to exhibit a poverty of both compassion and imagination. (Just as I cannot help fantasying about the effects on the prospects of peace if everyone who advocated war were automatically placed in a front-line rifle company on the outbreak of war, so I wonder whether megalopolis would have any advocates if every advocate were sentenced to spend a lifetime there.)

As a site for an association of self-governing citizens, megalopolis is a disaster. By preempting the place of a truly local territorial government, megalopolis prevents its inhabitants from being citizens of a true city (from Old French, *cite*, from the Latin *civitas*, originally citizenship, from *civis*, citizen, from which also, of course, civility and civilization). It is demonstrably true that sticks and stones may break our bones, but words can also hurt when names conceal realities. Because New York is called a city, its government must be a local government. Consequently inhabitants of New York City find it hard to demand, or even to realize that they have a right to demand, a genuine local government, a city where democratic citizenship is possible. Our little exercise in arithmetic demonstrated that in a city of 7 or 8 million even a highly visible mayor is bound to be inaccessible to most citizens. For most people, participation in governing megalopolis must necessarily be largely symbolic, as in the realm of a prince. To be sure, the prince may be benign. He may try to be responsive. He may consult a great many advisers. He may go so far as to invite the common people to his levees, or rather his promenades. But so long as he wishes to act like a prince, only a few people can participate much in his decisions. The irreparable defect of the principate is not in the prince but that he is a prince.

If the inhabitants of megalopolis were to think of it not as a local government but as a regional government, they would at once understand that they are entitled to participate in a local government. If New York City were to become a state, as I rather think it ought to, symbols would be closer to reality. It would then be perfectly obvious to the residents of the new state of Gotham that like many other Americans they ought to establish genuine local governments within the state. I do not argue that the task would be a simple one, but it would be so clearly desirable as to make movement in that direction irresistible.

At this point you are likely to object that any attempt to develop opportunities for greater participation in smaller territorial units is going to impale us on the horns of our dilemma. Can we find units of government that are small enough to facilitate participation and yet large enough to exercise authority so significant as to make participation worthwhile?

Neighbors

Since megalopolis is not going to vanish overnight, its citizens need opportunities to participate in smaller territorial units. Even in cities of more modest size, smaller subunits can contribute to a better solution to our dilemma.

The term *neighborhood* is frequently used for these smaller units within city or megalopolis, and I shall use it here accompanied by the warning that the word seems to have no standard meaning and is applied indiscriminately to aggregates that include anything from a few hundred people to more than a hundred thousand. There is no simple formula for "neighborhood government" or, as it is sometimes called, "community control." To develop satisfactory governments for these subunits is going to require a good deal of experimentation. One of the most promising solutions, though surely not the unique solution, is the neighborhood corporation, which residents of a particular area are entitled to join, thereby obtaining rights to participate in its affairs. A considerable variety of functions can be devolved upon the neighborhood corporation.

To middle-class residents of a suburb or a smaller city, neighborhood government might seem to offer little beyond what they already have. But among those who now have little influence, it could dramatically increase opportunities to participate in decisions. The main beneficiaries might therefore be the less well off strata, black and white, locked into slums and ghettos. Social scientists have accumulated an impressive body of evidence for predicting that many, perhaps most, of these people would not seize their new opportunities. Personal and political demoralization, apathy, cynicism, alienation are not going to be erased overnight by neighborhood governments or anything else. Yet it would be wrong, I believe, to deprecate the importance of developing governments more accessible and responsive to the politically weak simply because their initial participation would, foreseeably, be low. As I have already said in connection with self-management, if we were to abolish democracy wherever substantial segments of the population failed to use their opportunities to participate, there might not be much in the way of rule by the people left standing anywhere in the world.

Neighborhoods help to civilize megalopolis, and neighborhood governments will help to restore citizenship to the noncitizens of megalopolis. Yet government in the neighborhood will have to be pretty limited, because the decisions of residents in a particular neighborhood on a great many matters — police, for example, or housing, transportation, health, segregation, zoning, revenues, or even education — are bound to have highly significant consequences for residents outside the neighborhood. The Principle of Affected Interests, then, imposes serious limits on the autonomy and range of activities neighborhood governments should be granted — and, I imagine, will be granted.

This is no argument against neighborhood government. When democracy is conceived of as a set of Chinese boxes, it is an argument for seeing the neighborhood as a constituent unit within larger units. May there not be a unit larger than the neighborhood that could provide fuller citizenship for the subject-citizens of a polyarchy?

Citizens

I think that the optimal unit is, or rather could be, the city of intermediate size, bigger than neighborhood, smaller than megalopolis. Such a city could solve our problem better than either neighborhood or megalopolis, and better, surely, than polyarchy in the giant nation-state.

The problem arises, you will remember, because there is often a trade-off between opportunities for participation and the worth of participation. To insist too much on one may give us too little of the other.

An optimal solution might be a territorial unit where citizens have an opportunity to participate at a satisfactory level on matters important to them. I suppose an ideal solution would require that the matter be truly important to them — presumably in the eye of God, History, Science, or Idea. But I mean nothing so Platonic, simply what the individual feels to be important. And I would describe participation as satisfactory if every citizen who wished to could participate about as much as she wanted to, every viewpoint was pretty adequately represented in the process, no one who actively tried found decision makers inaccessible, and few if any citizens felt that people like themselves were denied adequate opportunities to participate. My optimum begins to look distant enough to please those who believe we should strive only for ideals that are unattainable.

The appropriate site looks to me to be a city between about fifty thousand and several hundred thousand inhabitants. Within this range the decisions (or nondecisions) of the city government cut pretty deeply into the daily lives of the inhabitants, and they could cut deeper still. Of course, any city in this range is already much too large for primary democracy or for any enforceable guarantee that every citizen could participate at every stage in decision making. But it is probably small enough for a satisfactory level of participation. Simply to help you get a feel for the size of it, reflect that if every adult in a city of 200,000 belonged to a neighborhood unit of about 500 people—a unit small enough for primary democracy—then every primary unit could be represented in an assembly of about 200. I offer this not as a recommended form of city government but as an illustration of how quick and easy political communication and action might be in a city of this size.

"That is all very well," you may say. "Perhaps effective participation on important matters is theoretically possible in cities roughly within the range you've been describing. But certainly effective participation isn't inevitable, or even common, in such cities. Just look around!"

The objection, alas, is all too valid. As a logician would say, smallness may be a necessary condition for effective participation, but most definitely it is not a sufficient condition. There is evidence that in the United States, the larger a community is, the bigger the proportion of its residents who have a sense of powerlessness and feel estranged from government. But I am not aware of any evidence demonstrating that, in general, residents of smaller cities participate more than residents of larger cities in governing. If smaller cities have a greater theoretical potential, as I have argued, for the most part it seems to be unrealized. Why?

To begin with, there are restrictions on opportunities to participate. Let me emphasize one more time—the last in these essays

—that until and unless we reach much greater parity in the distribution of political resources, other steps toward democratization are like treating tuberculosis with aspirin, or airdropping marshmallows to famine victims.

Even if there were no gross inequalities, the structure and practices of government in most cities inhibit rather than invite citizen participation. Traditional structures do not provide the ready access to expert know-how that is so often a prerequisite to effectiveness these days. "Modern" structures of city government are, if anything, worse, for the main aim of "modernizing" city governments for half a century has been to bring in, to protect, and to insulate the professional not only from the politician but also from the ordinary citizen. Look, for example, at any city planning department and you will see how totally self-enclosed it is, isolated from politicians, citizens, and the slightest influence of the course of events. It is heresy, or at least was until recently, to suppose that ordinary citizens might have something important to say about the planning and development of the city or their part of it.

As to the importance attached to the city's decisions, American cities are incomparably more autonomous and powerful than cities in centralized countries like France and Italy, where building a new school or adding a new course requires action by the central ministry; even so, it is only yesterday that U.S. cities began to acquire some of the powers they need to deal with their problems. They are still heavily dependent on state capitals and Washington. An advocate of the Chinese box interpretation of democracy can hardly advocate totally autonomous cities; yet the constraints on cities are excessive, a result of a long legacy of distrust of cities in legislatures that until a few years ago were often dominated by representatives of small towns and rural areas. The greatest inroads on the autonomy of the city result from its lack of financial resources. As everyone knows, its traditional source of revenue, the tax on real property, has long since been inadequate, and when cities turn for help to the state capital and Washington, they end up with closely supervised grants for specific purposes. The city will never begin to meet its problems or attain a satisfactory level of self-government until it has a generous and predictable flow of unencumbered funds — an automatic share of federal tax revenues, for example. Cities are not only pathetically short of money; they are short of opportunities to spend it as their citizens wish, foolishly if it comes to that.

Immense incursions into the autonomy of cities, and hence on the importance of the decisions they can make, also take place as megalopolis spreads. The more that urban sprawl makes urban residents part of one boundless megalopolitan jungle the more difficult it is for residents of any smaller part to cope with their problems in their own way. Interdependence is the enemy of autonomy. Some students of urban life claim to see already in being a megalopolis covering practically the whole Eastern seaboard. Some even celebrate its arrival as a new stage in urbanization. A new stage it surely is, in its own way as sinister and antihuman as the new stage of warfare heralded by the atom bomb.

Like oil spilling from some giant tanker, crippled and drifting, megalopolis spreads and threatens life. In order to halt and finally reverse the spread of megalopolis we would have to reject the American booster mania that blindly equates the better with the bigger, whether cars, office buildings, strawberries, or cities. We would have to plan consciously to prevent cities from growing too large and learn how best to do so. We would have to establish a vast program of creating new cities and in this way thin out megalopolis, replace boundaries of asphalt with boundaries of woods and fields, and learn what surely must be counted among the greatest of the arts — though it is no part of American tradition or consciousness — the art of building great, not giant, cities.

It is exactly there, I imagine, that we confront our biggest chance of failure. I do not see how we can do what needs to be done until an integral part of our culture and habits of thought is a vision of the potentiality of the city as a major civilizing force; a unit of human proportions in a world grown giant, demonic, incomprehensible; an optimal site for democracy; an education in the arts and habits of democratic life; an association in which citizens can learn that collective benefits from cooperation and peaceful conflict are so great that rational self-interest must act as a restraint on self-destructive egoism; an opportunity to engage in creating a new kind of community the shape of which no expert can foresee and to which every citizen can contribute.

We are very far from having such a vision, and the agony of our cities is so intense and could be so prolonged that if the vision ever comes to us we may no longer have the energy, the will, the confidence to act on it.

Still, if we were to begin now to do more than talk of the need for change or to speak facilely of revolution and think hard about the kind of society we want, there might be time enough.

So: we have moved from principles to problems to solutions. We have moved swiftly, perhaps too swiftly. There were places along the way, I imagine, which a skeptical and curious reader would want to—and ought to—explore more fully. I would be the last to argue that we have covered enough ground.

Nor would I hold up the sequence—from principles to problems to proffered solutions—as a perfect pattern laid up in some Platonic heaven, irreversible, like time's arrow. Though you would find it less tidy, it would not be absurd for you to start with your own proposed solutions and work backward. You might very well surprise yourself with the principles you found at the end, or would it actually be the beginning? In thought and rational discussion, we must move back and forth along this path, which is not straight but triangular, with sides marked Principles, Problems, Solutions, except that at any point you may and almost certainly will generate a new triangle.

Well, we really are at the end. Or the beginning.

NOTES

1. THREE CRITERIA FOR AUTHORITY

1 Robert Michels, *Political Parties*, with introduction by S. M. Lipset, trans. E. Paul and C. Paul (New York: Collier Books, 1962).
2 Nelson W. Polsby, *Consequences of Party Reform* (New York: Oxford University Press, 1983), p. 63.
3 This is, for example, Polsby's view. See ibid., esp. chs. 3–5, pp. 89–186.
4 *New York Times*, February 12, 1969, p. 14.
5 I examine them much more extensively in *Democracy and Its Critics* (New Haven: Yale University Press, 1989), esp. chs. 4–5, pp. 52–82.
6 *The Republic*, trans. F. M. Cornford (New York: Oxford University Press, 1945), pp. 262–63.
7 H. D. F. Kitto, *The Greeks* (Baltimore: Penguin Books, 1957), p. 126.
8 Ibid., p. 262. Jowett's reading of the passage in Book VII, 540, is: "Making philosophy their chief pursuit, but, when their turn comes, toiling also at politics and ruling for the public good, not as though they were performing some heroic action, but simply as a matter of duty." *The Dialogues of Plato* (New York: Random House, 1937), 1:799.
9 Robert C. Wood, *1400 Governments* (Garden City, N.Y.: Anchor Books, 1964), p. 1.
10 Committee for Economic Development, *Modernizing Local Government* (New York: CED, 1966), p. 12.

2. VARIETIES OF DEMOCRATIC AUTHORITY

1 R. R. Palmer, *The Age of the Democratic Revolution*, 2 vols. (Princeton: Princeton University Press, 1959), vol. 1, *The Challenge*, pp. 155–58.
2 Among these were the decision in 427 to condemn to death the rebellious Mytilenaeans, which, however, was reversed the next day; the shameful decision in 416 to exterminate the people of Melos, which to the everlasting disgrace of Athens was not reversed; and also in 416 the decision to send the expedition to Sicily, which was followed two years

later by a decision to send reinforcements rather than to withdraw. The Sicilian expedition might be characterized as Athens' Vietnam; but since it never recovered from the disaster, one hopes that, like most historical analogies, this one is imperfect.

3 Because readers of *The Social Contract* are sometimes confused by Rousseau's description of forms of government, it may be helpful to append a few words of clarification. Rousseau makes quite clear that no state can be legitimate unless the authority of the government is derived directly from and only from laws passed by the assembled people (*not* by "representatives"). The execution or administration of these laws, however, could be delegated to a single person, a minority of the people, or the whole people. Rousseau chose to call the first "monarchy," the second "aristocracy," and the third "democracy." He recognized that the conditions under which a people could both make its laws and administer them as a body were so rare as to make "democracy" (in his sense) virtually impossible. "If there were a people of gods, they would govern themselves democratically. A government so perfect is not appropriate for men" (Book III, Ch. IV). In fact, none of these pure forms, according to Rousseau, existed or was likely to exist in practice. "It is necessary that a single head have subordinate magistrates; it is necessary that a popular government have a chief." Thus in practice most governments would be mixed (Book III, Ch. VII). Presumably all these forms of government could be legitimate; the crucial point to Rousseau was whether or not they derived *all* their authority *exclusively* from laws passed by the *assembled people*. It is in this sense that Rousseau is an advocate of what a few pages back I called primary democracy. The term is mine, not his; what Rousseau calls democracy I would call a variant of primary democracy. It is a variant so extreme in its requirements that Rousseau can hardly be said to advocate democracy in his sense. If democracy as Rousseau himself defined it seemed impossible to him, primary democracy as I have defined it seemed to him not only possible and desirable but the *only* kind of legitimate state.

4 Palmer, *Age of the Democratic Revolution*, 1:118.

5 Ibid., pp. 127–39.

6 Ibid., p. 128. In *The Social Contract* Rousseau mentions with astounding complacency that in Geneva there are four orders of men ("even five, counting ordinary strangers") "of which only two make up the Republic" (Book II, Ch. VI, n. 1). The fact does not seem to disturb him.

7 *Capitalism, Socialism, and Democracy*, 2d ed. (New York: Harper, 1947), p. 245, n. 13.

8 Rousseau regarded Corsica with special affection. "I have a presentiment," he wrote in *The Social Contract*, "that one day this little island will astonish Europe." He was right, of course, but for the wrong reasons.

9 Alvin M. Weinberg, "In Defense of Science," *Science* 167 (9 January 1970): 145.

10 It is hard to know whether Rousseau really thought he had a way to get the genie back into the bottle. A few chapters earlier (Ch. XIII), he says that if it is impossible to reduce a state to small enough limits, the solution is to move the capital alternately from one village to another. Thus the people of each village would be "sovereign" in turn. It is curious that he does not balk at this arbitrary solution when he so strongly objects to the selection of representatives by election or by lot.

11 C. Vellay, ed., *Discours et rapports de Robespierre* (Paris, 1908), pp. 324–28, quoted in Palmer, *Age of the Democratic Revolution*, vol. 2, *The Struggle*, p. 115.

3. DEMOCRACY AND MARKETS

1 Karl Polanyi, *The Great Transformation* (New York: Rinehart and Co., 1944).

2 Charles E. Lindblom and Robert A. Dahl, *Politics, Economics, and Welfare* (New York: Harper and Brothers, 1953; reprint, with a new preface, Chicago: University of Chicago Press, 1976).

4. FROM PRINCIPLES TO PROBLEMS

1 The sociologist Robert K. Merton has called this "the Matthew effect." "The Matthew Effect in Science," in Robert K. Merton, *The Sociology of Science* (Chicago: University of Chicago Press, 1973), pp. 439–59.

2 See Charles Lewis Taylor and Michael C. Hudson, *World Handbook of Political and Social Indicators*, 2d ed. (New Haven: Yale University Press, 1972), Table 4.13, pp. 264–65.

3 Even before a major revision of American income tax rates in 1986, which markedly reduced taxes at the higher levels, an authority had written: "Contrary to popular belief, the federal individual income tax

does not exert a major effect on the distribution of income in the United States. . . . Under current law the individual income tax reduces the before-tax area of inequality by 4.61 percent." Benjamin A. Okner, *Income Distribution and the Federal Income Tax* (Ann Arbor: Institute of Public Administration, 1966), p. 6. The same study shows that among those who had enough income to file a return, under 1965 statutory provisions the richest 10 percent received 31.3 percent of the total income before taxes and 29.4 percent *after* taxes, while the poorest 30 percent received 11.4 percent of total income before taxes and 12.3 percent after taxes. Ibid., Table D.1, p. 131. In 1986 the poorest 40 percent of American families received 15 percent of the aggregate income of all families, the top 20 percent received 44 percent, and the top 5 percent received 17 percent. U.S. Bureau of the Census, *Statistical Abstract of the United States, 1988*, 108th ed. (Washington, D.C., 1987), Table 701, p. 428.

4 Quoted in Joseph Pechman, *Federal Tax Policy* (Washington, D.C.: Brookings Institution, 1966), p. 179.

5 Report of the Joint Economic Committee of the U.S. Congress, *The Concentration of Wealth in the United States* (Washington, D.C.: Joint Economic Committee, July 1986), Table 2, p. 24.

6 Richard Barber, *The American Corporation: Its Power, Its Money, Its Politics* (New York: Dutton, 1970), p. 184.

7 "Today the gross sales revenue of the top twenty or so American companies is equal to Britain's GNP. Belgium's budget could be financed from the profits of just America's top four firms." Ibid., p. 257.

8 *An Inquiry into the Nature and Causes of the Wealth of Nations*, 7th ed. (London: Strahan and Cadell, 1793), p. 96.

9 See, for example, Eric Rhenman, *Industrial Democracy and Industrial Management* (London: Tavistock, 1968).

10 Barber, *American Corporation*, p. 97.

11 Ibid., p. 98.

12 That Americans persistently prefer living elsewhere than in cities is shown in surveys from the 1960s to the present. For example, in 1987 among a random sample of 800 residents of New Jersey, only 10 percent said that living in a city was very desirable, compared with 38 percent, older suburbs, 50 percent, small towns, and 34 percent, rural areas. Moreover, 67 percent said living in a city was *not* desirable, compared with 17 percent, older suburbs, 16 percent, small towns, and 30 percent, rural areas (Eagleton Poll, August 1987). A decade earlier, among

a national sample, only 13 percent said that if they could live anywhere they wished, they would prefer a city over 100,000; 29 percent said they would prefer a small city (between 10,000 and 100,000); 20 percent preferred a town or village up to 10,000; and 38 percent preferred a rural area (The Gallup Poll, *Public Opinion* 1972–1977 [Wilmington, Del.: Scholarly Resources, 1978], 2:914). See also Gallup Political Index, March 1966, p. 23.

13 Studies have failed to turn up any significant economies in city government attributable to larger size. The few items on which increasing size does lead to decreasing unit costs, such as water and sewerage, are too small a proportion of total city outlays to lead to significant economies. Even these are probably offset by rising costs for other services, such as police protection. The writing on this matter is extensive, but the most relevant studies are cited in my "The City in the Future of Democracy," *American Political Science Review* 61, no. 4 (December 1967): 953–70, esp. 966, n. 14.

14 Cf. Wilbur R. Thompson, *A Preface to Urban Economics* (Baltimore: Johns Hopkins University Press, 1965), ch. 7.

INDEX

Administration, need for, 72–73
Affected interests: principle of, 49–51, 102 ff.; and management of firms, 113 ff., 121–22
Aristocracy, problems in, 27 ff.
Aristotle, on equality of resources, 90–91
Assembly, Athens, or *ekklesia*, 30 ff., 53–54
Associations, consensual. *See* consensual associations
Athens, democracy in, 30–31
Authority: three criteria for, 6 ff.; varieties of democratic authority, 45 ff.; delegated, 59
Autonomous decisions, or Consumers' choice, 15, 16–21

Barber, Richard, 97, 110–11, 149
Berle, Adolf, and Gardner Means, 104
Boulê. *See* Council of Five Hundred
Brogan, Dennis, 93
Bryce, James, 90

Capitalism, capitalist economies. *See* Markets
Chinese boxes, 68 ff.
Cities: populations of, 128; optimum size of, 132
Collective decisions, 15
Competence: as criterion for authority, 21–30; moral, 21; and

personal choice, 23–25; and political equality, 25 ff.; of ordinary people, 26; and aristocracy, 27; summary, 29–30; departures from, 88; and business firms, 96 ff.; and selection by lot, 124
Consensual associations, 14, 16–21
Consociational democracy, 17
Consumer sovereignty, 15
Corporations, corporate leviathan, 96 ff.; as private enterprises, 100; government of, 101 ff.; self-management vs. interest group management, 107, 114; and competence, 109 ff.; and personal choice, 111 ff.
Corporatism, democratic, 84–85
Council of Five Hundred (*boulê*) in Athens, 30, 59
Crèvecoeur, J. Hector St. John, 90

Delegation, delegated authority, 59, 69, 72, 75
Democracy: forms of, 52 ff.; committee, 52; primary or town meeting, 52; representative, 55 (*see also* representation); referendum, 55; amateurs and professionals in, 58; participatory, 62; dilemma of primary democracy, 63; democratic corporatism, 84
Democratization: Greece, Rome,

143